Spirit Things

Alaska Literary Series
Peggy Shumaker, Series Editor

ALASKA
LITERARY
SERIES

The Alaska Literary Series publishes poetry, fiction, and literary nonfiction. Successful manuscripts have a strong connection to Alaska or the circumpolar north, are written by people living in the Far North, or both. We prefer writing that makes the northern experience available to the world, and we choose manuscripts that offer compelling literary insights into the human condition.

Spirit Things

LARA MESSERSMITH-GLAVIN

Illustrations by Roger Peet

Alaska Literary Series
University of Alaska Press
Fairbanks

© 2022 by University Press of Colorado

Published by University of Alaska Press
An imprint of University Press of Colorado
245 Century Circle, Suite 202
Louisville, Colorado 80027

 The University Press of Colorado is a proud
member of Association of University Presses.

The University Press of Colorado is a cooperative publishing enterprise supported, in part, by Adams State University, Colorado State University, Fort Lewis College, Metropolitan State University of Denver, Regis University, University of Alaska Fairbanks, University of Colorado, University of Northern Colorado, University of Wyoming, Utah State University, and Western Colorado University.

∞ This paper meets the requirements of the ANSI/NISO Z39.48–1992 (Permanence of Paper).

ISBN: 978-1-60223-455-0 (paperback)
ISBN: 978-1-60223-456-7 (ebook)
https://doi.org/10.5876/9781602234567

Library of Congress Cataloging-in-Publication Data
Cataloging-in-Publication data for this title is available online at the Library of Congress.

Interior illustrations by Roger Peet
Cover photograph © kavring/Shutterstock

For anyone who lives between worlds.
You know who you are.

Contents

Spirit Things

AN INTRODUCTION

I HAVE AN OBJECT that leans on the windowsill in my kitchen. It's a rusty oval, with a frayed knotted hitch cinched at the top. It looks industrial, weathered, esoteric. It is roughly the size of my hand. If I hold it up, it frames my field of view like a cameo brooch, but with the discarded charm of a junkyard find. For years, I wore it around my neck as a pendant on a length of leather, but now it just graces my sill, having aged from totem to knickknack.

This oval was once a metal ring that held the end of a rope that had been carefully spliced around it by hand. It once served a purpose, holding fast, transmuting the rope into a line to do a very important job on a fishing boat. The metal was exposed to sunlight and salt, grew dusty and corroded along its pores. The circular ring elongated over time, stretching into a narrow egg, describing exactly the tension it had borne and the strength of its material. Its deformation was like a poem of strain and circumstance, its shape a perfect overlap of utility and form. It is not the shape itself that is beautiful to me; it is what the shape tells me about its history, that the story is there inside of it if I know what to look for.

I like things—which is not quite the same as liking *stuff*. I don't enjoy shopping or collecting; I don't accumulate items on purpose. I am drawn to objects with stories inside them: the bowls my great-aunt used to make bread, the pocketknife my father uses to clean his nails, the pencil that inexplicably becomes my favorite despite no apparent difference other than that it's the one I always choose. When we live with things, imbue them with use and care, when they become extensions of our bodies to work, to create, to touch the world, they take on their own quiet power. I like magical objects and the histories they carry inside of them.

What is the difference between a history and a story? Is a history somehow more fact driven, a story more open to embellishment? The ways histories are used to shape thoughts in favor of one perspective over another suggest otherwise. Communities and cultures have histories, as do relationships or technologies. Lovers have histories. We can talk about the history of Greenland, the history of the cotton gin, the history of salt. I suppose a history is more about a shared experience—How did we get here? it might seek to answer. Why are we in the situation we are in? A story, on the other hand, may be private. A story draws its reality from the ways it plays inside of us, reflecting truth off our inner surfaces, shaping our feelings as well as our facts. We tell ourselves stories about who we are, about what happened to make us so. Our stories are symbols, signposts, examples or warnings of how to be. We are raised on histories and stories both, some clunky and deliberate like the ones we drag from textbooks, while others are furtive and hidden, like seeds planted without our knowing, recognizable only when they bloom.

I had an unusual upbringing. My parents were commercial fishermen in Alaska, but we lived elsewhere the rest of the year, in southern Indiana until I was in the second grade, and then eastern Oregon until I left for college on the East Coast. This meant I moved back and forth between worlds, leaving every summer for Kodiak and then returning for school every fall. One was the boat world, wet and loud and full of work. It was edged with danger, and its seasonal community offered a kind of tough frontier spirit in lieu of a culture. The other world was landlocked and dry, miles of flat, cornstalked stillness or rolling tan hills roughed with sage. The land world held friends, school, ways of playing. In the boat world, I had only grown-ups. In place of playmates, I had direct contact with the wild: salmon and halibut gasping for breath, skittering crabs, the rich scents of jellyfish and seaweed. There were roaming bears, eagles as common as pigeons, and the ocean, always the ocean, tossing and leaping and murmuring beneath me.

As I was an only child, it was a very solitary way to grow up, even if it wasn't exactly lonely. It is very difficult to be alone on a fishing boat. It did mean, though, that much of my early years were spent investigating and thinking by myself while my parents were on deck. Even as I grew older, I was the only person my age, which meant that, even in the company of the crew, I was often a community of one.

It was rare that we stopped fishing to socialize or explore, but it did happen on occasion, when the season would close temporarily, and all the gear work and repairs were taken care of. Once, we anchored up off Spruce Island and took a skiff to the beach, where we were met by an old friend, a Native boatbuilder named Ed Opheim. He took us to his workshop, a graying barn at the edge of the woods where the earth met the sand, and he gave us a tour of his handiwork while he and my father swapped fishing stories. Stepping inside was like entering a museum of magical things. Myriad mysterious tools cluttered his workbenches, old metal in different shapes bound with handles of wood and cloth and plastic, different edges for prying, for peeling, for coaxing, for gouging, for pounding. Curls of wood were scattered like confetti, mounds of sawdust gathered in drifts against every upright surface, as if there had been a tiny, festive storm. The space was rich with the golden scent of raw lumber, the heady lurk of epoxies and fiberglass. In the center of the shop sat a beautiful hull, a wooden craft in the process of coming into being. Its lines were still blurred, not yet settled into their final shapes, but it was already so suffused with its boatness that it practically trembled, anticipating the water beneath it. I ran my hand along its side like I was calming a large animal, feeling the grain of the wood in its skin. Ed smiled, interrupting his reminiscence to acknowledge me and my attention to his boat.

"You need to write the stories, Lara Lee," he said. He was talking about fishing, not about the boat itself, but I was only eleven years old and all of these things were one thing for me. "You're the youngest person who remembers the way it used to be."

At the time, I felt both intimidated and thrilled at this thought, and I accepted the charge solemnly. I have carried it with me since, even though I don't know how it used to be for others, or what the *it* really was. I know the way *it* was for me—which is probably quite unlike the experiences of other deckhands, or of boatbuilders, or of the Native communities. Mine is the perspective of a child, a teen, an adult looking back and tracing the impacts of that time on my life and identity. Now, when people ask me about Alaska and what it was like fishing—especially in the heyday of the 1980s—I think what they're hoping for are salty sea stories, filled with outlaw characters and colorful language. Some have watched shows like *The Deadliest Catch* and are riveted by the vicarious thrill of danger, the potential for disaster. The human connection and the characters, the relationships, the drama—those are the histories, I suppose. For those, people should listen to my parents share their memories, the parade of specifics and timeless quotes that come from a lifetime spent fishing. They have those pieces of history. Mine are something different.

Stories are what build our sense of meaning in the world; they're what reveal the magic and change inside all things. In the shifting, seasonal culture of the fleet, there were few storytellers who offered me these meanings. There were elders, and I listened to them gratefully and hung on their tales of giant halibut coming over the side, of being knocked overboard by a crab pot and living to tell the tale, of pulling in nets by hand. As I began to call forth stories of my own, however, I found that what I wanted to talk about were objects. I don't recall the name of a particular boat or remember the politics of a sudden closure, but I remember with stark clarity the way the windows would crust with salt from the spray that leapt up the sides of the boat as we traveled. I don't know why we fished in one place rather than another—I was a child on deck, following orders, not making decisions—but I can tell you exactly how the twine was wrapped around the handle of the white knife we used to hack the kelp from the net.

How do we tell our own stories when no framework has been given for deeper meanings? How do we create a cosmology of our own? In the absence of storytellers, wise women, or a culture of collectivity, I had things and feelings, my senses, and an overwhelming contact with the ocean, a living symbol of the messiness, the terror, the creativity and beauty of the divine. Each object in this book has taught me something about the world: how to occupy it, how to behave in it, what to expect from others, people and non-people. Each object has its own kind of magic. I decided to let these things be my storytellers: the nets, the knots, the gloves. I sat down and asked each of them, "What did you teach me?" Whether history or story, this is what they said.

2

Net

I.

AS A CHILD, I marveled at the heaps of seines that lined the docks on pallets, like the necklaces of a giantess piled along the boardwalk. The black web was strung through with playful colors, edged with frayed splices and thick lines of turquoise and yellow and pink, beaded with rounded floats in brown and algaed white. I loved the smell of them, the sour salt and fish reek, the tar and cork. Dried jellyfish hardened to gooey jewels in the mesh. I loved clambering on the piles, the dense way they absorbed my punches and jumps, their warm heft when left in the sun, like patient animals. It was clear to me then, as now—nets are a form of magic.

For one thing, they move between worlds. The net is a creation from land that serves no purpose there. Its only function is to extend the grasp of drylanders: once submerged, it becomes a ghost of the fisherman's will haunting a domain where the fisherman cannot dwell. It allows water to pass through it as if the net were not even there. It is meant to deceive, and then to trap. Its purpose is to visit, to take, and then to return to land with other things that do not belong there, things from the underwater world.

This in-betweenness gives nets a certain power. In folktales, when fishermen cast their nets into the ocean, they often pull up wonders in place of their catch: talking fish, strange babies for barren mothers, enormous pearls, loaves of bread. It is as if the very act of straining the water is an incantation or spell—the uncertainty of the sea itself a thing of stories. As sorcerers must ask for help from untrustworthy spirits, when we fish for our own gain, we do so by crossing that watery barrier, and invite risk and visitation of the unknown.

Superstitions abound to counter those risks. Some are simply rituals to summon prosperity or show gratitude to whatever gods or giants may control the realm—like kissing the first salmon caught in a season and throwing it back overboard. Others are wards against misfortune, many of which are so old or have traveled so far from their origins that their true purpose is lost. Bananas are forbidden on boats, for instance, as are suitcases, women, and whistling. Never leave port on a Friday or change a vessel's name. These sound arbitrary, mere folk charms from quainter pasts, but many are still obeyed without question. It is difficult to know which gods may be listening or watching in any given waters, so most mariners simply prefer not to take the chance.

II.

For the old Norse, the giant Ægir was responsible for the benevolence of the sea, the bounty they drew from it and the beauty that formed the horizons of their world. His daughters were the Nine Waves, each named after an aspect of the ocean's surface. They were lovely and nymph-like, dancing on the surface of the ocean, laughing and tossing at the edges of the Vikings' ships. In the eddas, thirteenth-century manuscripts that captured much of Norse mythology, the sea giant and his daughters personified the Nordic wonder and familiarity with the water, their love of its facets and changeability. But the mother of the Nine Waves, Rán—it was she who brought the storms.

Rán, the Cold Queen, embodied the dark indifference of the ocean, the bitter violence that pitched ships about on open water and tore them apart against the rocks of the coasts. It was she who waited for raiders and fishermen alike, holding a net of her own, tossing it from the deep and dragging men overboard, calmly pulling the drowned men downward into her bed. It was this net that the men feared, more than the crashing seas or weather. Ægir was unpredictable and powerful, but Rán was a ravager, greedy and beautiful, filling the halls of Ægirheim with her collection of dead souls. A raider who died at sea would not end up in Valhalla with his friends from battle but would feast and couple with Rán until she tired of him, at which point she would cast him to Helheim, the Land of the truly Dead. Rán's underwater appetites were known to be fickle and unquenchable, rivaled only by her craving for wealth. For this reason, Vikings often went to sea with gold coins in their pockets, tokens to offer her, either tossed overboard as a bribe for safe passage or as a means of bargaining for mercy, seeking to please her for as long as they could, should she tangle them in her nets and draw them down.

Translations of Rán's name differ, but many suggest that it means the "Robber," as she took from mariners and raiders and coastal folk alike. In Alaska we drew our wealth from the sea as well. Instead of pulling men down, we pulled salmon upward, drowning them in the air. They flopped and kicked as men do below, desperate gills flailing to draw breath. The sound of their thick bodies striking the deck was like wet applause. Gradually, their movements subsided into occasional, spasmodic claps until at last they lay still, shifting in flat unison with the rock of the boat. Thousands of them would pile motionless in the fish hold. Over time, the rhythmic movement of the swell would settle them all tail-down, their faces frozen upward in open-mouth gasps, their eyes dead ohs of horror. Their death became our gold. I sometimes imagined them whispering to me, offering supernatural trades for their lives: *Three wishes—if you'll only throw me back.*

III.

On a seining boat, the net is heart of the operation. The main boat holds one end in a curved shape while a small skiff runs to the beach with the other, and together, they hold the net like a wall in the water, blocking the way for salmon trying to return home to their streams. The fish are pulled by the necessity to spawn and then die—when they encounter a barrier on their way, they will instinctually seek deeper water, heading seaward as if to navigate a rock or cape, but once there, they find the net hooks back around them, and they become confused. The fish swim in circles until the two ends of the net are brought together and the bottom is pursed up, catching them in a bag that is eventually pulled on board. As deckhands, our job was to stack the net carefully—the cork line that makes it float piled on one side of the deck, the leads that make it sink on the other, and the vast curtains of dark web in between.

A seine is a miracle of mathematics, sequences of squares that compress and balloon and create lines and curves out of straight edges and angles. My father, a tall, white-bearded man who could easily pass for a minor sea giant, taught me just how to hold it as he mended the holes that rocks or gear had torn into it. I held the net at the corners of the squares, creating tension as he tugged with the big needle that held the twine, gathering folds of web to offer as he moved to the right or the left. He formed loops with practiced speed, measuring them with his fingertips as he went, cinching each with a knot that would not slip under pressure. He tied diamonds of twine that, once in the water, would relax into squares and stretch out, forming an underwater sail.

The magic of sewing web is that sometimes in order to fix a hole, you first have to cut. Greenhorns shake their heads—how can a knife fix a tear? And yet that is how it works. We cut and cut, sometimes along an entire length, looking for the end of the hole: the three-bar, it's called, a place where the edges of the diamonds lined up side-by-side rather than point-to-point. Once we found the three-bar, we could build it back up, moving at a diagonal along the web rather than straight across, more knitting than building.

I would hold up the corner, and he would tie off with a starting knot. I held tight and pulled back hard against the yanks that seized the knots. The twine would pop off the edge of the needle with a round *tok* sound I could feel in my mouth. I watched the diamonds form, the web a dark puddle at our feet. We could not track our progress by seeing as we mended; we trusted that the shapes were correct, the measurements intuitive and exact. Along the length of the tear and back, back and forth, he would rebuild the web. When we came to the end—another three-bar—he would tie it off, and we would drop the net. The hole would be invisible, as if it had never been there at all. Like magic.

IV.

The most ancient evidence of fishing nets comes from Antrea, Finland, in a region now part of Russia. The Antrean net was probably around thirty meters long, with mesh measuring six centimeters across. I imagine it looked much like the tightly sewn scraps of herring seine we used as hammocks and storage slings for gear, only woven of willow and floated with pine, ten thousand years before our synthetic webs. When the net was discovered (by a farmer, tilling a field that hadn't been a lake for thousands of years), other bits of tools and weapons made of stone and bone were found, suggesting the fisherman's boat had capsized. To whom had that fisherman prayed then, when the waters came over the side? What story helped him understand his end?

The earliest recorded Finnish lore says that a violent, moss-bearded god named Ahti presided over the deeps of oceans and lakes in a war gown made of sea-foam. It was Ahti who would usher the fish into one's net, or herd them out if he were angry. He was said to be brooding and gloomy, bound to the waters, jealous of the sky gods and their dry and airy ways. His wife, Vellamo, was known to control the winds to help sailors, and was favored by fishermen for her beauty. However, she broke a promise she had made to Ahti, one that kept him home safe and barred him from raiding. She sent him out into battle, and he fell in combat upon the sea. When his body sank into the ocean, did the fish feast upon him there, or did he become part of the waves to lash at the rocks, the jealous spray never quite touching the sky?

Around the world and throughout history, there are few stories in which the ocean is simply a benevolent spirit, a thing of beauty, a resource. Behind all of its faces it is capricious, violent, gorgeous, and indifferent. It is a wild place, one humans visit at their peril. And like death, it is both unknowable and commonplace.

Fishermen dip their nets into those waters as if reaching across that barrier of knowing. Just as the stories of the sea and its movements capture terror and power in human terms—jealousies and lusts and restlessness—so are the nets our feeble attempts to draw from our own depths, to capture those mysteries and wrap them in words. What is pulled gasping ashore are old and wild things, monsters, oddities to be marveled at and consumed. Yet our casting in dark waters requires a trade, and gods rarely give up their secrets on purpose. We are left with dead specimens, rocks and clods of underwater clay, tangled balls of kelp. Sometimes our own refuse returns to us, mangled and bleached. What we drag up tells us nothing about the foreign movements of the true deeps, the dance and tilt that happen under the surface. Likewise, the body of a fish, caught lifeless in a diamond of web, reveals nothing of its darting, driven self.

3

Salmon

I.

THE SALMON SLIDES OUT of the can in a solid chunk, making a wet snick as it falls into the metal mixing bowl. The ripples from the can are imprinted in the packed flesh, and I can see the part where the skin is still on, the spinal cord popping apart in pieces. I wince as the cat food smell drifts down to me.

"Gross," I mutter.

My mom ignores me, busily working the fish into smaller, uniform chunks with her hands, crushing the vertebrae between her fingers and mixing it into the rest.

"It's calcium. It's good for you," she says, not looking down.

From my angle, I can only just see into the bowl. My mom rinses her hands at the sink and tosses a handful of green onions onto the cutting board, *tak tak tak* they become uniform little rounds and are scraped with the blade of the knife on top of the salmon. One— two, she cracks eggs over the fish, swearing under her breath as she digs out a piece of shell with a fingernail. She flings in spices, imprecision being the soul of her culinary art. Salt and pepper, something in a plastic bottle with a yellow cap that I recognize—we use it on the boat for a compress when we're stung by jellyfish—then herbs that she digs from an unlabeled jar that she's sniffed to identify, all sprinkled liberally over the lot. Three shakes of hot sauce. She washes her hands again.

"Is that it?" She looks at me to see if I remember the recipe.

"Breadcrumbs," I say.

"Breadcrumbs." She disappears behind the swinging pantry door and rummages among our dry goods. I hear her knocking things off shelves, the hiss of bagged bulk items—rices, beans—sliding in their baskets. She slams through cupboards with the unselfconscious loudness of the hard of hearing, returns to the counter holding not a cardboard breadcrumb can but a white plastic sheath of crackers.

"Those aren't breadcrumbs."

She smiles and opens a drawer, handing me a rolling pin.

"This is more fun. And we don't have any breadcrumbs anyway."

"Saltines are fun?"

"Yes. Saltines are fun. Just watch."

She produces a large Ziploc bag and dumps in the whole mess of crackers, carefully squeezing the air out before zipping it shut. She unceremoniously tosses it onto the counter and takes the rolling pin from me, banging at the bag like she's trying to kill a particularly large spider. When she's reduced the crackers to wreckage, she hands me the rolling pin again.

"Want to?"

I begin rolling the bag vigorously. The crackers make a satisfying sound as I go, first crunching like gravel, and then snow, and finally like gritting over fine sand. I plow over them until my arms ache from reaching up to the countertop, and all that's left in the bag is a fine salty dust.

"That should do it," she says.

She shakes the contents of the Ziploc into the mixing bowl and mushes it all together with her hands, kneading it as if it were pie dough. She forms it into patties and fries them in oil in a huge cast iron skillet, gently placing each onto yesterday's classifieds to drain once it turns a perfect golden brown. I try to peek at the stove but am popped in the nose by the hot oil. The smell is amazing. My mom hustles me out of the kitchen, only to return with a small plate holding two hot salmon cakes and a fork. I take the plate and drown them both in ketchup, then retreat to the living room, in front of the

TV, where reruns of *The Dukes of Hazzard* are playing. I don't really like salmon cakes, but mom says they're cheap and healthy, and we eat them often, which only embarrasses me when friends stay the night. Other kids get hotdogs. I get canned salmon. I crunch against a bit of bone and grimace, spitting it out on my plate. It's so much better straight from the net.

II.

The salmon in that can was processed in a cannery that lies at the mouth of Larsen Bay, which is situated inside the much larger Uyak Bay on the Alaska island of Kodiak, the first and largest of the Aleutian chain, stretching westward. The cannery sits on its inlet with its back to the ocean, gazing inward at its own little bay as if it were the entire world. The spit of land reaches out and holds the cannery on its spindly piling legs as if cradling the water, keeping it calm and glassy even when whitecaps churn and rage on the open seas beyond. The hillsides slope rapidly downward, choked with *pushki* and fireweed, green and blazing purple in July, after the sockeye runs are strongest.

The cannery has had many different names and owners over the years—Icicle, Kodiak Salmon Packers, Larsen Bay Seafoods. In all its incarnations, it has been a microcosm, isolated from the outside world and even from the local Native village, population forty-two in the most recent census, located only half a mile away up a gravel road. In the 1980s and '90s, the cannery was flooded with itinerant runs of young white folks, seeking seasonal jobs in the summers and returning to college in the fall, though now the workers include people of all ages from around the world. The cannery is also home to a handful of year-rounders, hardened crew who keep the machinery working and the young folks from killing themselves through sharp injury or drowning. It often boasts the odd mascot—a few white-muzzled dogs, a friendly office cat, once a blind gray pony that lived tethered to an A-frame just off the dock. Occasionally, the grizzlies wander down from the dump and are shooed back into the hills with clanging pots and pellet guns.

The buildings are all the same weathered blue-gray, the color of wood that's met the sea. The rooftops are pale yellow blooming to rust red, and the boardwalk, a pointed finger of planks reaching outward into the bay for fishing boats to tie up, smells of tar and salt. The planks themselves are worn and splintery, like gnawed bones, but their undersides are dark, as are the pilings that hold them up. The pilings are slick with tar that protects them from the daily rise and fall of the tide, tar that looks black but stains your fingers yellow if you touch it. Knots of mussels and barnacles cluster up their surfaces. Climbing a ladder at low tide from a boat to the dock is like seeing two sides of the world: the shadowy below is dim and teeming with life. Narrow shafts of light slip between the boards and pierce the vibrant dark of the water, where diesel blooms rainbows across the surface and wavelets lap. Emerging onto the dock, the bleached sun side is sere and dull, a worn path leading straight to the cannery proper.

Each building has a single purpose—one is a web loft, where fishermen who sell to the cannery store their nets. One is the boiler room, where enormous tanks pressurize and cook cans of fish. One is a mess hall. Others are bunkhouses, rickety temporary homes for the workers, each named after a Native totemic animal—Raven, Puffin, Wolf—as if the entire affair were a summer camp and not a commercial processing plant. There are separate bunkhouses for the Japanese workers, small crews who speak little English and keep entirely to themselves, whose sole job is to harvest and inspect the roe, or *ikura*, from the pregnant female chum salmon, and gather it, primarily, for a single festival in Japan. Their building is called The Spring House. It sports a faded red sun on the dangling wooden sign above the door.

During lulls or closures, times when the Department of Fish and Game shut down fishing grounds to allow runs to return, the cannery is silent, abandoned-feeling, like a shell of an industry long obsolete. During openers, when the fishing grounds are busy, it has the vivid tension of a hive—rushed and hectic, with workers and forklifts buzzing at all hours. The beep and roar of skidloaders drown out the repetitive clang of machinery; seagulls and terns cry overhead.

Cannery work is hard. It runs on a feast-or-famine cycle of heavy runs followed by closures or periods of no fish, and the cycles are not always easy to predict. People work all hours offloading tenders, running the "slime line," where fish are cleaned and decapitated, and operating the cannery itself, where the product is packed into cans and then cooked, sealed, and left to cool. Everything is slippery with gore, water, and gurry; the days are long and irregular; there are sharp things clanging and slicing and belts and hydraulics inexorably churning at every turn. Injuries happen. One man in a tuna cannery in California was even locked inside a boiler on accident and cooked alive. Everyone works hard to stay awake, and safety precautions are drilled into second nature.

The work is punctuated in turn by the hoot of whistles calling everyone to mug-up, the mandatory break periods when mess workers bring out steaming canisters of hot chocolate and coffee, trays of cinnamon rolls, baskets of donut holes. The slime line crews and the drivers clutch steaming mugs and lounge in their yellow raingear pants, hair tied back in bandanas. They laugh and joke or catch precious moments of shuteye, leaning against a stack of pallets. The Japanese workers sit a distance apart, their sleeve protectors and shining black rubber boots still on. They smoke and watch the water with passive, disinterested faces. They seem not to notice the rest of the crew.

The pace and physical seclusion of the work make for a rare form of camaraderie for most. Impromptu basketball games break out on the dock during free time. Beaches are combed. Friendships with fishermen form during closures, or when boats come in to do gear work or engine repair. These connections often result in drunken deck parties, skiff rides across the bay, or explorations in search of legendary *banyas*, makeshift saunas hidden near streams in the wilderness. Bonds formed here between workers are strong and often last long past the summer. At the same time, the isolation of the cannery can wear on the nerves. Long lines form outside the small row of pay phones. Long-distance calls home cost fortunes—where else can the money be spent?—and last hours, evidenced by the intricate carvings on the bleached wood walls of the phone booths.

Janet and Caleb 4-ever.

Coming Home 2 U—in the penknife edges of a jagged heart.

My parents worked in a cannery together when they were first married. My father worked the beach gang, hauling gear and doing heavy physical labor. My mother worked the slime and canning lines. She still recalls the conversations she and the other women would have through the long, repetitive hours spent on the line. They would talk and laugh together, their soft voices meeting somewhere under the din of the machinery. They described fantasies, meals they missed, dates they'd been on. What will you do when you get home? What kind of music makes you dance? If your breasts were birds, what kinds of birds would they be? Hens, doves, wrens.

My mother was hard of hearing then; she is nearly deaf now, no doubt due, in part, to the constant wear of mechanical noise. But she took sensual pleasure in many aspects of the work. When I was a child, long after she had stopped working in the cannery and she and my dad had moved on to fishing and owning a boat of their own, she would take me through it as if visiting different kingdoms of the senses. We would enter the egg house and pry open small wooden crates stamped with Japanese characters to taste the salty red pops of roe. We haunted the web loft, with its thick ocean smells of dried kelp and tarred twine, its airless hush. She showed me the can house, where we would run our hands over the warm metal, guessing how long they'd been out of the boiler, and then sit still and silent, listening to the cans cool. It was magical—a secret thing, the way the lids would pop when the change in pressure pulled them into themselves, a small symphony of voices erupting all around us. *Pop. Ping.*

III.

The salmon in that can that was processed in Larsen Bay arrived at the cannery via a tender. The tender is a larger boat that acts as a shuttle between the cannery and the fishing grounds, carrying product from the fishing boats to the processing plant so the fishermen do not waste time traveling back and forth. Most tenders are cannery-specific, so one opening or fishing ground may have several tenders anchored nearby, waiting for the boats loyal to their affiliated company to deliver their fish at the end of each day.

As a go-between, the tenders also serve as a connection to shore in other ways. They bring supplies to the boats—fuel, fresh produce, mail—and so serve a social purpose, as well. They are the human link to sustenance: food, diesel, but also news, cookies, sometimes—hallelujah—a shower, a precious commodity rarely experienced on a fishing boat, where fresh water is scarce and must be carefully rationed. Some specialty tenders even provide luxuries for their boats; the F/V *Balaena*, an old navy scow that had been repurposed for processing and tendering, was large enough that it held not only showers but a saltwater hot tub belowdecks and a soft-serve ice cream machine. The Cadillac of tenders.

Before the advent of pumps, fish delivery consisted of emptying a fish hold by hand. After tying up to the tender at the end of a day of fishing, the crew would don red pitching gloves that had the equivalent of rubber gravel covering their surface to ensure a decent grip on the slippery bodies of the salmon. They would then jump into the hold, regardless of how full it was—this could be up to their ankles or up to their necks—and begin tossing fish into a brailer, essentially an enormous mesh bag with a bottom that pursed and released, that was lowered from the tender and attached to a scale held by both boats' hydraulic pulleys for maneuverability. Different species of salmon—sockeye, coho, pink, chinook, chum—are each valued separately and so have to be sorted for weighing and pricing. Deckhands kept count as they pitched, sorting on the fly by looking at tail shape and characteristic markings that identify each species. As a small child, my job was to lean over the side of the hold with a metal click-counter in my fist, ticking off each fish as it went into the brailer so we could estimate size from the total weight.

Good deckhands could pitch two or more at a time and spot the difference between a king and a red at a glance; slow deckhands or those who made mistakes in identification, especially in favor of the tender, were ridiculed and badgered until they became faster and more accurate. Once I started working on deck at age eight, I learned to pitch as well. Instead of jumping into the hold like the grown-ups, I had to climb down by stepping on the corrugated metal slats that separated the subcompartments and kept salmon from sloshing back and forth in rough weather. More than once, I slipped and landed on my back on the cold, slick piles of dead fish, feeling their bodies shift beneath me as the gurry ran into my boots. I was an unbearably slow pitcher at first, a burden on the crew, and my father—the skipper—would jump in the hold to take up my slack. As I got older, I got faster and made it my personal mission to throw twice as many fish as any deckhand. We would have races, challenging both endurance and accuracy of identification. The first to throw a hundred fish would slap the others with dead pinks, covering their gear with blood and slime, or count aloud the number of extra fish pitched to make up the slower numbers. A big catch could mean hours of pitching at the end of an already long day of work. A good day often meant moving as much as two or three tons of fish per person into the brailers after fourteen or more hours of stacking the net. Sometimes it took so long that, as soon as the catch was offloaded, the boat would have to turn right around and head back out to the fishing grounds as the purple glow of the midsummer sky broke golden around the edges. There is little rest when the fish are running.

Once pumps were introduced in the mid-'90s, the process became much faster. Instead of individual brailers being lowered, filled, raised, weighed, then dumped into the tender's hold, a fat hose is now pushed into the fish hold and the salmon are essentially vacuumed up, then pumped onto a sorting table on the deck of the tender. The crew stand around the table and wait for the pump to disgorge sluicings of gurry and salmon, waterfalls of dead fish and pink foam, slime, and silver scales. They grab the fish from the sorting table as they slide past, tossing them into the appropriate brailers on deck, which are then weighed and dumped as before. Often, the tender crew will help sort, which makes the process even faster. I met one of my best friends this way, in my teens. Sorting takes less effort than pitching, which left room for awkward conversation. To help pass the time, I tried offering a bit of trivia I'd picked up from listening to skipper banter on the radio:

"Did you hear Jerry Garcia died?"
The tender hand blinked. "Who's Jerry Garcia?"
I liked him instantly.

No money exchanges hands in these transactions between boat and tender. The prices for fish fluctuate over the course of the summer, based upon run returns and other market forces, so selling for any given price at the moment would be like wagering on gas or betting against the future. Instead, the weights and species and price per pound at the time are noted, along with any subtractions for fuel or groceries purchased, and then the tickets are traded in at the end of the season for a massive lump sum once the final price is set. In this way, the paper the tickets are written on is worth more than gold. I remember my father leaping from deck to deck with the ticket in his mouth sometimes, and the look of panic that would cross his face if he temporarily dropped it.

There are also tenders called "cash buyer boats," which are rov-
ing tenders that often do not work for any given cannery. Instead,
they pay cash for the fish on site and bet against the market, hoping to make more by ranging from cannery to cannery and selling
at the best possible temporary price. These cash buyers carry enormous amounts of money in safes onboard and are generally very well
armed. They were the source of many pirate fantasies among my
crew. We would often spend free time plotting late-night attacks on
these boats to steal their cash. We once had a record-breaking haul
of silvers—120,000 pounds—which we sold to a cash buyer on site.
They paid my dad in thick rolls of stiff $100 bills, which he promptly
stuffed into a wool sock and buried under a bottle of gin in a drawer
in his stateroom. When the cash buyer anchored up yards away in
the bay hours later, my dad spent a sleepless night envisioning the
tender's crew, guns in hand, slipping quietly aboard our boat to take
the money back.

Tendering is easier work than cannery life or fishing, and so
it often has the reputation for being for families, old folks, or lazy
people. The interior of a tender told you a lot about the kind of
operation it was—some were pigsties, full of empty bags of chips
and beer cans, sporting Hustler pinups stuck to the wall with duct
tape. Others were clearly homes away from home, filled with family
photographs, the smell of freshly baked bread, and maybe a small
dog or a boat cat. Yet others were the rarest but the best to find—
the poet types, with tenders that also served as miniature floating
museums, graced with lithoprints in the galley and fresh flowers on
the table, art books lying about the cabin among the charts and tide
tables. These tenders would lend out months-old copies of the *New
Yorker*, ragged and folded at the corners, and offer small gifts of civilization: a baggie of ground espresso beans, a sip of good whiskey
from a mug, a book. They reminded us that there was still a world
outside, other things to think about besides spotting jumpers and
keeping our socks dry.

IV.

The salmon in the can that was processed at the cannery after being traded from boat to tender got caught because it jumped. It made the mistake of expressing its excitement at being in a large school of other fish, running together under the surface toward their spawning grounds. It gave away its location and that of its school. No one knows exactly why it happens—some theories suggest they are ridding the body of parasites; others say they just feel stressed or happy—but most species of salmon, when traveling in groups headed homeward, will occasionally leap out of the water and come back down on their sides in a bright silver smack.

Splash.

"Jumper!" I shade my eyes past the brim of my hat, squinting at the glare on the surface of the water. I feel the throttle of the boat slow. My dad must have heard me.

"Where?" he shouts. I point.

The rest of the crew is now staring at the water in the same direction—my mom, the other deckhand, and the skiffman at the stern, who never leaves the skiff until we're done for the day. It's quiet but for the constant underlying rumble of the diesel engine, the lap of the waves, the rhythmic creak of the lines above us straining as we rock.

Splash. Another jumper. Where there's one fish, there are more. Where there are multiple jumpers, there are lots.

Splash.

"Get ready!" my dad shouts from the flying bridge.

I pick up the small sledgehammer we use to unhook the skiff and stand at attention in front of the release. The skiffman revs his engine. I'm no longer watching the water, keeping my eyes instead on my dad, waiting for his signal. He pops his finger into the air.

"Let 'er go!"

I slam the sledgehammer into the pelican release, and it makes a loud, satisfying clang as the two lines separate. The skiff engine roars, and the smaller boat immediately wheels around and powers away, hauling one end of the net with it. I quickly climb off the stack and drag my end of the skiff line with me, unwrapping it from the winch and coiling it neatly off to one side of the deck. At ten years old, I have sets of tasks I am expected to do and do them perfectly and with speed.

Ten is a little young to be a deckhand, but it's not uncommon with family operations. I've been on the boat every summer since I was two, spending most of my time entertaining myself in the galley while the grown-ups worked. Then, when I was eight, one of our deckhands got caught selling weed over our boat's radio during a big opener and then borrowed the skiff to visit his girlfriend on a tender and forgot to bring it back in the morning. I learned a lot of new vocabulary from my dad that day. When one was fired, the other deckhand quit, and they both took a tender back to town. The trip from the fishing grounds around Kodiak Island to town takes sixteen hours traveling eleven knots an hour by boat—the runs were so huge, rather than waste time finding new crew, my dad put me on deck, stacking the corkline and doing the best I could with other jobs. My mom and dad did everything else until the run ended and there was a closure so we could go back to town and get another deckhand. If I could do it at eight, I could do it at nine and now ten, so I just stayed on deck.

The net is stacked neatly on the back deck: on one side the cork-line is piled in careful loops; on the other are the colorful mounds of heavy leads, the black mesh of the web piled in between. The skiff is only about fifteen feet long, an aluminum dinghy roughly the size of a car, snugged tightly to the stern between sets. When it separates from the boat on my release, the skiff takes one end of the net with it, stretching the seine out in the water to trap the fish, the corks floating one edge and the leads sinking to the bottom. The skiff has a shallow draft, so it holds its end as close to the shore as it can get. The surf is enormous there, and the skiffman hangs on with every swell, smashing against the beach with the bow and throttling hard against the undertow. On the boat, which is fifty-two feet long and floating on a much deeper hull, we move perpendicular to the shoreline, making a wall in the water with the net. The net is a quarter mile long, so it takes a few minutes to get the entire thing off the boat each set.

As the net leaps off the stern, the corks make a galloping sound, and bits of kelp and jellyfish are flung every which way. Every time the seine goes out, I watch all my work go in reverse and briefly remember each toss of the corks, all that labor unraveling. The skiff recedes into the distance, traced back to the deck by a bobbing dotted white line, all that is visible now of the seine.

The boat slows. The line holding our end of the net slithers off the deck and goes taut above our heads, and the seine is laid out. The clasp pops as it rotates and settles into towing the net. It's under tremendous pressure. The line itself is so tight that a deckhand can do a pull up hanging off of it, but it isn't a good idea. If that line goes, it would snap backward with enough force to take off a person's head. Or at least that was what my dad has warned me.

The bare deck is covered in sea trash left behind by the seine: knots of seaweed, hunks of clay, jellyfish, the occasional crab that minces toward a scupper and escapes. I pull on the yellow overalls of my raingear.

Everything on a boat is under tension—lines and hydraulics and people. I'm learning to listen to directions and respond without question, to keep myself and others safe. Every set, I go through a checklist in my mind about what has to happen next. If I can anticipate things, do them before I'm asked, nobody gets yelled at and things go the way they should. Sometimes it's hard just to remember the names of things, this line versus that line, let alone knowing what to do and how to do it and when to just get out of the way.

My next job is to flip the switch that turns on the seawater pump and then hose off the deck so it's clean. There's a great satisfaction to this—rinsing and chasing bits of detritus and blood and fish scales from the bulwarks and the surface of the deck, herding them with the jet of water into orderly streams and then swooshing them out the scuppers. The deck is painted a pale gray with grit in the surface for surer footing. Even though the net is about to come right back in, having a clean surface helps keep us from slipping as we work.

Now I have to plunge. The fish swim along the coastline in a more or less straight line. When they encounter the net, they will move seaward. The skiffman says they've learned that this is the way around other barriers, like rocks and sandbars. That means they'll move away from the skiff at the beach and toward our boat. We want to scare them back toward the beach to trap them, and so we use a plunger and whack the water at the stern. The plunger is a long aluminum pole with a cup on the end—when you slam it into the water, it pushes a pocket of air down beneath it and makes a wonderful *thock* sound, followed by a bellow of bubbles. My mom says the fish think it's a seal diving into the water to eat them, so it frightens them away. When I was six or seven, my dad made me a plunger pole out of a broomstick with a cork on the end, so I could help scare the fish. At ten I'm big enough to use the real thing. My shoulders ache from thocking at the stern, and I switch hands over and over. Sometimes the plunger misses the air pocket and makes a slushing sound instead, which isn't nearly as satisfying.

We turn the bow of the boat back toward the beach and maintain this position for some time—"holding the hook" for twenty minutes, half an hour. This is my favorite time of the set. The net is out, the deck is clean, the engine purrs, not roaring or racing, as we jog along. Nothing is going wrong yet.

It's a nice day. The other deckhand stays busy with little tasks, filling seine needles, sharpening knives. My mom brings me a mug of hot Tang and takes the plunger for a while. She wears her hair tied back in a bright bandana, and her orange gloves have smiley faces Sharpied onto the backs. She has a rainbow fish scale flashing on one cheek, and I reach up and peel it off. She takes it from my finger and presses it back onto her skin.

"My sequins," she says. I smile and drink my Tang, squinting against the glare on the water.

My dad and the skiffman stay in communication via radio during this time, watching for jumpers and streaks in the surface of the water and other indications of the movement of fish. Sometimes they talk in code so other skippers don't know how well they're doing. I think they're just making it up.

When they're satisfied that the bulk of the run is in the net, or when they can no longer see sign of anything, my dad gives the signal—making a hoop with his arms overhead—and shouts, "Close 'er up!" The skiff turns from the beach and begins making its way back toward the boat, hauling the other end of the net behind it. As the skiffman's features start to become clearer, those of us on deck hustle to get the rest of our gear on, sliding into the clammy jackets of our raingear, checking the small knives we wear taped to the suspenders of our rain pants, pulling on the wet, gooey gloves we wear while stacking the net.

When the skiff is in range, the skiffman tosses us the monkey fist, a complicated knot at the end of a smaller line that makes it easy to throw. He yanks the release and we pull in the line as fast as we can. Everything then has to happen very quickly. The deckhand draws up the end of the net and connects it to a line leading over a hydraulic pulley—the block—over our heads, then opens the valve that starts it turning and begins pulling it downward to begin stacking the net on the back of the deck. My mom runs to the other side of the deck and throws the towline to the skiff, so he can hook up near the stern and begin pulling the boat around the quarter-mile fish corral the net now makes in the water. My dad shimmies backward down the ladder from the flying bridge with his back to the rungs, facing the deck, and puts a hand on the hydraulic controls. I grab yet another line and race up the narrow edge of the boat alongside the cabin to the bow. I tie the bowline off on a cleat, whipping it into figure eights and then flipping the last few loops under themselves to seize under tension, and then run back to the deck, balancing along the railing of the bulwarks.

On deck, things have gotten very loud. Over the roar and gurgle of the skiff's engine and jets, the hydraulics hum and whine, and seawater patters across the hold as the net is hauled up from the water at an angle over the block and then pulled downward into a tidy pile. The web slips and screeches overhead—it isn't moving as it should. My mom and the other deckhand loop their gloved fingers into the mesh and heave downward, trying to muscle thousands of pounds of gear over the hydraulic pulley. I leap over the fish hold and jump up into the cascade of net, grabbing on with both hands and dangling, trying to add my weight to the effort. If it is snagged and fails to gain traction, it could slip all the way backward and we could lose it off the side—opening the corral and releasing the fish. If one of our hands were caught in the web when that happened, we'd be dragged through the block and torn in half by the pressure. My mom says she wears gloves to protect her hands from rough surfaces. My dad says we wear gloves so that we have something to take off if we get snagged in the web. Better to lose a glove than a hand.

"Pull, goddammit!" My dad leaves his place at the hydraulics and grabs a chunk of the lead line. We all strain together, and, slowly, the net gains traction in the block overhead and begins to fall smoothly. Unlike the crew, who live in their oilskins, the skipper doesn't wear raingear unless the weather requires it, so now his jeans and fleece are soaked through in places. He makes an impatient patting gesture at the skiffman that means slow down and glares out at the net, daring the fish not to be there.

The rest of the set goes as it should. My heart races nonetheless; I'm always afraid of making a mistake. It's partly about not getting hurt, but it's also about money. Based on watching other fishermen, it's hard to tell which is more important. I focus on piling the corkline so that it will uncoil without binding or lumping when it goes out again. Water streams down my arms from the net every time I reach upward to grasp a new bight of the corks coming down from the block, and my sweatshirt sleeves are soaked beneath my gear. Mountains of dark web tumble down in the center of the deck, and my mom bats it into place, meanwhile tugging out large snarls of seaweed and hurling them overboard, or plucking out gillers, salmon that have been caught in the mesh by the gills. She tosses these over the corkline onto the hatch at my dad's feet. The deckhand on leads keeps one hand holding tension on the lead line, which purses the bottom of the seine into a bag. If it slips, we lose the purse. With his other hand, he tosses the rest of the leads into tidy back-and-forth stacks on the side of the boat where the net is coming in. His hood is up to protect him from the constant rain of water and jellyfish that pours from the web over his head. Mine is up, too, but there is less to worry about on the dry side of the deck, except for the bits of stinging jellies that are flung sideways in the process of stacking or blown into my eyes and across my neck by the wind.

As the circle of the net draws closer, it becomes shallower, and the fish inside become visible, agitated. The water is dark and alive, shot through with darting shadows and choppy on the surface. Once we get to the end, the bottom of the seine has completely closed up, forming a large bag that shudders and froths, full of frantic, flapping fish. There are thousands—mixed species, a pain to sort while pitching, but typical for this time in the season when all kinds are running. My dad whoops and grins, and I jump over the stack to help him drag the hatch covers off the hold. The hydraulics strain again as the bag leaves the water, and we all heave on the net as the bag slowly drags over the side. My dad leans into it, guiding it over the hold, and then releases his end of the purse line. The bag spills open and thousands of fish pour out everywhere—mostly into the hold, but also ankle-deep across the deck, their bodies clapping and slapping, swimming on their bellies across the hatch. We quickly pull the remainder of the net over the block, being careful not to get hit in the head by the heavy metal clasps at the end. The entire operation, from release to hauling the bag, has taken about an hour. We immediately reset so we can do it again. We'll probably make ten sets today, maybe more if they keep running like this.

My mom turns to catch the painter line from the skiff and hooks him back up. The other deckhand is already looping the tie-up line around the winch and easing it up with the hydraulics. I grab the block line and run it up to my dad, who cinches it and clambers back up the ladder to the flying bridge and the controls. I turn and begin tossing salmon into the hold, one by one, two by two if I can get them by the gills. They fight and flip, spattering my face with gurry and scales. Some nearly flop themselves back overboard to freedom. We move as quickly as we can, tossing them into the hold. Their bodies are strong and heavy and fiercely alive in my hands. It is impossible not to admire these fish. It's a strange feeling, having so much admiration for a creature you have just killed.

V.

The salmon that was running along the coastline until it encountered our net had been trying to reach the very stream where it once hatched. Salmon are born in rivers, make their way to the sea, and then return to their same rivers to spawn and die. After spending eighteen months in the ocean having successfully avoided being eaten by sea lions, humpback whales, sharks, and halibut, this fish, a pink salmon, became inexorably drawn to the freshwater stream where it first emerged from its redd, or nest, as part of a complex cycle of endurance and transformation.

Salmon roe are perfectly round, smaller than peas, the color of fire. They are hidden by their mothers like clusters of jewels, tucked into pockets of gravel in a riverbed. Once fertilized, they must survive predation by animals and other fish, as well as freezing, overheating, and suffocation from silt in the water, or disturbance of their redd. When they hatch, the alevins—tiny little fish still carrying their yolk sacs—remain in the gravel and under rocks until they are ready to find food on their own. They emerge from the redd as fry, slightly larger fish, dodging insects and birds and hiding in the pockets of shadow created by stones and fallen tree branches. Some species of salmon remain in their river or nearby lake for years, growing larger and developing strength and scales for ocean waters. Pink salmon, however, quickly become silvery smolts and begin making their way downstream to the ocean.

As smolts travel seaward, they form schools. Some fight their way down the river, swimming vigorously, while smaller smolts turn tails forward and simply allow themselves to be pulled by the current. Though camouflaged with striping that mimics the sunlight bending through the stream, they often travel at night, avoiding otters and eagles and other hungry river creatures. During the days, they depend upon the safety of shadows, hiding places, and their sheer numbers to survive.

Once they reach the estuary, where ocean and freshwater mix, they spend some time adapting to the saltwater chemistry and eating as many tiny fish and insects as they can, developing strength to live in the open sea. Their bodies undergo amazing transformations to allow them to enter the saltwater environment—changes to their kidneys, to their gills. They develop specific markings according to their species: striped tails for chums; thick, speckled tails and black mouths for kings; spots on their backs for pinks. When they are ready, the school enters the ocean and eventually disbands, though they often stay close to shore for a time, where coastal rock formations provide some safety.

Adult salmon live at sea for some time—years, depending on the species—and can travel hundreds, and in some cases thousands, of miles to reach feeding grounds. Biologists call this "movement ecology," an adaptation where a species is capable of roaming great distances in search of more suitable environments, seeking food and shelter and avoiding predators or changes in climate or other seasonal conditions. Salmon are nomads and survivors. They eat smaller fish and live largely solitary lives until nature whispers to them that it is time for them to return home—and die.

The anadromous instinct pulled this pink salmon back to the sheltered fresh water of its original river. But how does it do it? How, after years and hundreds or even thousands of miles, does a salmon find its way home? Some biologists think it has to do with the salmon's sense of smell and with unique chemical combinations in the water. Other scientists think it's related, in part, to the position and angle of the sun.

Another possibility is that salmon, like sea turtles—another marine animal that finds its way home over thousands of miles—are sensitive to unique patterns in the Earth's magnetic field. It is as if the field itself creates an invisible grid around the planet, a chart constructed of intersections of unseen details—field intensity, angle of inclination, perhaps—that the fish are able to navigate to return, over great distances, to their natal streams. Using metallic bits in its nose called magnetoreceptors, the pink salmon—the one that was caught in a net, delivered to a tender, transported to a cannery, gutted, processed, canned, shipped, and, ultimately, fried into salmon cakes with saltines—swam through hundreds of miles of ocean, following a hidden map of magnetic bends and imprints. It is possible that this fish knew, always, where it was—in the sea and in relation to the freshwater gravel bed where it first emerged into sunlight.

Due to predators—orcas, sea lions, humans—many salmon never have the opportunity to complete the cycle. Those who do arrive at the mouth of their home river must begin the long fight upstream. Contact with fresh water brings about another set of transformations—the fish stop eating and begin to lose muscle mass and fat. Their colors darken, and males develop large humps or hooked noses, which they use to fight one another for dominance. Moving against the flow, they battle currents and shallows, leaping over rocks and struggling against the rush of fresh water. Many become too exhausted to finish the journey. Some are blocked by dams or other obstructions, and others are eaten by bears or eagles along the way. Those who make it all the way back to their original streambed create redds of their own, filling them with thousands of eggs or fertilizing them. After spawning, both males and females soon die, their bodies undergoing yet another change, returning nutrients to the river where their roe lie in wait for spring.

VI.

The salmon that we caught, sold, processed, and ate is the hero of a story that is thousands of years old. The relationships between salmon and people have been examined for generations, appearing in the myths, artwork, and cultural products of most Indigenous nations of the Pacific Northwest. Because of the richness of the salmon runs prior to white colonialism, the salmon represents prosperity and bounty. Due to the complex and multistage life cycle the salmon completes, it also symbolizes goals and determination, intuition, renewal, and transformation. Images of the salmon appear in basketry, paintings, lyrics, carvings, clothing, dances—and stories.

The Haida have lived in the Pacific Northwest coastal region of what is now North America for over 12,500 years. They were there when the first tree arrived, according to both oral histories and pollen records. They observed the patterns of salmon, the mysteries of their wayfinding and shapeshifting, the power of their instinct long, long before Seward's Folly or commercial salmon fishing in Alaska. The Swimmer, they called the salmon and passed along stories of the intimate link between humans and fish.

The Haida tell of a youth called Salmon Boy, who was disrespectful and did not treat salmon with care. He would catch and eat fish and then toss the bones into the bushes or kick carcasses of the dead. His elders warned him to honor the fish, but he would not.

One day, as he was swimming in the river with some other boys, he was caught in a current and carried away from them. He wasn't a strong enough swimmer to keep his head above the surface. The river eventually pulled him under, and he drowned. As his body remained trapped, he found he was still swimming downstream, running with the Salmon People, who were taking him with them to the ocean and making him one of their own. They were leaving their streambeds without their bodies and racing to the sea as spirits, where they took human form and returned to their village—which looked very much like his own village, river and all—under the waves. There, the boy lived with them and learned from them. They taught him the ways the Salmon People left their bodies behind in the rivers for the Human People and other Animal People—Bear People, Eagle People—to use and then return.

He found himself hungry one afternoon, and the Salmon People told him to go to the river behind their village and catch one of their children for him to eat. There, he found salmon swimming in the stream, and carefully, he drew one out and prepared it as he was taught. When he finished eating, the Salmon People instructed him to place all the bones back into the water—that way the child could return to them whole, in spirit form and in body. He did so, but when the children came home from swimming, one was crying because it couldn't walk. One of her feet was missing. The boy quickly found a small bone he had forgotten to return to the river, and once he placed it into the running waters, the girl was healed.

The boy spent the winter in the ocean with the Salmon People, and in the spring, it was time for them to return to the rivers. When he swam past his old village, his own mother caught him in a net and fished him from the water. She recognized her son, even though he was in salmon form, by the copper necklace he wore around his neck. She had given it to him as a gift, long ago. Gently, she carried her son home and held him for days as he slowly shed his salmon skin and his human form reemerged. The Salmon Boy shared all he had learned with the people of the village, offering healing and counsel, and begged them to remember his teachings.

After the salmon had all returned up the river to lay their eggs and their dead bodies had begun to drift again downstream, Salmon Boy went to the edge of the river and gazed down into the water. The ragged, decomposing body of a salmon floated past, and he recognized it as his own spirit. He thrust his spear through its tattered, spent sides, and there he died on the banks of the river.

Following his teachings, the people of the village carefully placed his salmon body back into the water and watched it circle slowly, then sink, knowing it would one day return. The spirit of the Salmon Boy raced downstream, back to the ocean, eager to join his People.

Note: The Salmon Boy story is one of the oldest in the region. Among the Tlingit, the story is claimed by the Kiksádi, L'eeneidí, and Lukaax̲ádi clans. While I was unable to determine the exact clan origin of this Haida version, I want to acknowledge its claim by the Central Council of Tlingit and Haida Indian Tribes of Alaska. I encourage anyone who is interested in the story to investigate the resources included in the references regarding how the Salmon Boy story is taught and shared.

4

Wave

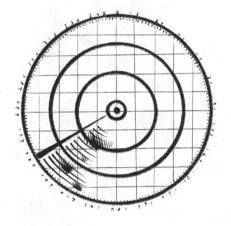

IN THE HEART OF SUMMER IN ALASKA, night never really gets dark. The sun slowly lolls to the horizon and dips under, briefly. The colors drain from the sky, leaving the world in blurry, two-tone shadows of bone and violet. As a child, I learned to sleep in the light, and fear of the dark was never a big part of the formation of my world or my place in it.

When I was very small—three until six or so—my bed on the boat was in the stateroom with my parents. They had a double-wide bunk that packed them both in like sardines and left me with nowhere to go but up. They hung a length of fishing web from strong hooks screwed into the walls above their bunk and tossed a sleeping bag into it, creating a makeshift hammock that swung back and forth with the swell. It gently knocked against the walls in calmer seas, my body a metronome ticking off each rock of the boat. The balanced touch of that—a tap on the left, a tap on the right—was comforting. When it was rough, the hammock moved violently, unpredictably, and I would brace myself with my hands or feet, jamming them against the stateroom walls at stiff angles to keep from slamming my sides against them. At one end of the bunk was a locking window that looked out over the water. Waves would smash against it and drain away, leaving the view spotted and cloudy with salt during the day. At night, the midnight sun bled purple against the stateroom walls.

By the time I was too long to fit comfortably in a hammock, sleeping feet above my parents was awkward for everyone. Plus, I was a deckhand by then, so I was sent to sleep with the rest of the crew, in the fo'c'sle (forecastle, pronounced *folk's hole*). The fo'c'sle was a dark den inside the bow of the boat, through the galley. The walls curved downward, following the shape of the hull, and their sides were cov-ered in thick shag carpet, an odd addition to a place that was often wet. It was damp and full of smells—days'-old fish gurry and unwashed men and boots left on—but it also had the closest approximation to darkness, and I slept burrowed against the inner hull, my exhausted hands absently stroking the carpet and tangling in its long fibers.

When we anchored up at night in a bay or lagoon, protected from the swell, I would listen to the water lapping against the fiber-glass hull by my head. Some nights the gentle slosh and lick was another comfort, a rhythmic patter like slow rain. But most nights, that sound whispered to me, invoking darkness far denser and fright-ening than the sky could hold. It was a cold sound, a reaching one. Every wavelet felt like a hand snaking up from the depths to taunt me, striking against the hull right where my face, my torso and limbs were on the other side. Rather than reminding me of the safety of the boat, the sounds at the waterline accentuated the thinness of the barrier between my body and the impossible depths that lay below it, as if the waves were only toying with us, great hands gently rolling an egg back and forth between their palms. At any moment, they could crush our protective shell at will. *Slap. Slosh-slap.* Those sounds pulled me to sleep at night, downward, so that rest became an act of surrender to a great, bottomless fear.

Why is vastness so frightening? In daylight, gazing out over the water at the horizon, I often felt a sense of power and calm. The water stretched to the edge of the earth and then fell away with the curve, describing the limits of the world in perfect silver lines. This view engendered awe, a great feeling of fullness and tranquility. But when I allowed my mind to sink below the surface, to try to comprehend how far the water went downward, the awe twisted in on itself and turned dark and terrible. It was too much to hold, that depth. To my child mind, the waves became the reach of the deeps, reminders that I floated on the upper edge of an unbearable abyss. We lived in a liminal zone between an ever-bright sky and a dark horror of water.

Maybe it was just a fear of drowning—my body was just a tiny bit of flesh adrift on a little machine in a great expanse—yet the survival of my physical self felt like the least of my worries. Something about contact with that magnitude of size put my sense of soul at risk. It was a different *kind* of drowning that was at stake. It reduced me to panic more than once, trying to hold the ocean in my mind. Once, when I was five or six, I was practicing. I tried to fill my vision with the surface of the water and then let myself imagine downward, to see how far I could go. The next thing I remember, I was shaking as if I'd been plunged into ice water, shrieking, "I don't want to die! I don't want to die! I don't want to die!" My parents were confused and frightened, my hysteria sudden and strange in a child. My mom held me on her lap in the stateroom, rocking me back and forth, echoing the swell of the boat. My dad got angry; there was no time nor room in his world for attacks of the infinite. He called me "ridiculous," and stormed out.

It was many years before I learned to put up barriers between myself and this terrible feeling of limitlessness. I learned to ride out that sense of totality, to watch how others understood things, how they dealt with size and terror. People protect themselves from immensity by breaking it into smaller bits—types, categories, tendencies. Instead of beholding an abyss, people divide the ocean into currents, bays, trenches. The vastness is charted and plumbed. By converting it into the knowable, the predictable, the fear transmutes into respect. By naming it, the relationship with the infinite is tamed back to a bearable awe.

~

The old Norse were some of the most successful seafarers the world has ever seen. They made it from Europe to North America long before Columbus, they navigated without sextants or chronometers, they traveled hundreds and sometimes thousands of miles in small, open ships, often without prior knowledge of their destination. How did they overcome fear?

One way was to tell stories. Most of what is known about their stories comes from the Poetic Edda, Icelandic poems recounting much of the spiritual life of the old Norse, pre-Christianity. Prior to that, outside of the occasional use of runes, Norse culture relied upon an oral tradition, skalds crafting poems to please the kings and chieftains of the time, the winners rewriting history in the moment. In this tradition, the lives of gods and giants and those of people were interwoven, the sacred and the mundane one and the same. They gave voices and reason to the forces that molded their experience—to lightning, to crop failure, to capsized ships. These poems also acted like teaching tools, passing down the frameworks and details and values they wanted to endure. The Edda was finally written down at a point when the stories themselves were centuries distant, and Christianity had provided a new lens for the gods and goddesses and giants of their myths. This means these poems are re-creations of the original culture at best—perversions and fantasies at worst—yet that is the period in which the Norse became truly literate, so that is the version that survives. Whether spoken or written, within the poems are repetitions, clues; within the myths and stories, the knowledge of the world itself, a reflection of what is known about the seasons, about weather, about battle and love and the sea.

For the old Norse, the ocean was not the domain of a god or goddess but rather two giants and their children. Ægir, the sea giant, represented the glory of the water, both the benevolent beauty of the ocean and its changeability, as he was given to moods. He was known to be a generous host and often entertained the gods themselves in his great underwater hall, Ægirheim, a reflection of the ocean's bounty the Norse enjoyed and their dependence upon fisheries for food. His wife, Rán, was the darker aspect of the sea, the destruction and loss it could wreak. She provided a focus for their fears, and in naming her, they gained a feeling of control over their fates.

Ægir and Rán also had nine daughters, known as the Nine Waves. In the names of the Nine Waves, an intimacy with the surface of the water itself is revealed, a knowledge of what it can be and how it moves. Each name is representative of a different kind of wave, a way of passing down close observations of the ocean and its many faces.

Hevring was the riser, the wave that lifted the boat high and offered a view of the horizon and the coming swells. Hrönn was a welling wave, the kind that rolled for miles and brought rhythm and number to their rowing or the brace of their legs. Dúfa was the pitching wave who tossed their boats unpredictably from the surface only to have them slam back down again into the water, shuddering and creaking, like riding the back of a great beast.

There were also Bylgja, the billowing wave; Uðr, the frothing one, whose whitecaps indicated wind or choppy weather; and Kólga, the cool wave, whose cold hands and kisses soaked through the sailors' rough-spun garments and left them heavy and shivering on deck. Close to shore was Dröfn, the foam-flecked, or comber, crashing against rocks and beaches. They also named Blóðughadda, Bloody-Hair, who bore the deadly color of red tides and shark bites. And lastly was Himinglæva, the wave through which one glimpses heaven, when the sun pours down and shatters against the surface of the water, when all the horizon becomes piercing light.

These were the faces of the sea for them, names for the many ways the immensity appeared—the motions of the waves, the waves that sighed against the sand, the waves that tapped the hull, the waves that smashed ships apart or carried them to unknown shores. Naming them turned them into intimates, lovers, enemies. Personalities to watch for, patterns to predict what happened next.

When I see the surface, I see chop, swell, breaker, trough—but mostly noise. I see things moving and changing. I see the differences in shapes, but I don't know what I'm seeing, what they mean—about the currents and changes and depths of which they are the signs. I cannot read their faces. I wish I'd had stories to give meaning to the waves, to render them familiar.

Would the vastness feel less frightening if I had the words to name the shapes? Even if the language were all my own? *Seeker*, I would name the lap at my head. *Whisperer*. I would call the flat erasure of our wake *Scar*, with its curious smoothness like skin healed strangely after a wound. The giant, tossing seas would be *Rage*—there was such hideous power in the way they threw us about, out of our control but also out of its own, in the way that anger overpowers the spirit and gathers force and wildness to it, feeds with irrational speed on its own heat. *Serpents* would be the fingers of water that rush up the sand on the beach and the hissing undertow that pulls them back. I would name the salt spray that stings the eyes *Needle*, and the looping ovals of bright and shadow that swirl on a calm sea would be *Boil*. There are many others whose names I could give, but far more who remain strangers to me, whose aspects are lost to my poor understanding of the ocean as a whole.

In the northern reaches of the Arctic, far beyond the outline of Kodiak Island that I both knew well and didn't know at all, the Inuit people have found their way through snow and sea fog, through seemingly endless and featureless landscapes too close to magnetic north to trust a compass. They have done this in part through intimate understanding of the land and its inhabitants—the sounds of wind, the patterns of current and snow drift, the behaviors of animals, the smells. *Aangaittuq*, they call those who navigate well, "attentive." And this attention is cultivated and taught as an attitude and way of life, not just as a skill set used to find one's way home after hunting. Navigators are seen as cultural teachers; they often spend times of rest helping novices practice describing locations, orienting themselves and others through a collective understanding of place.

There are many ways of codifying shared knowledge and passing it down, both metaphorical and real. My family and other deckhands taught me to recognize where there may be fish, to know which way the current is running by watching the surface of the water. I was taught to spot jumpers and be vigilant for rocks. I can read tide rips, shallows, and schools of salmon. I never learned to anticipate the interaction of swells, to predict the weather by watching the waves or the sky. I cannot gauge depth, or track the stars, or find my way across a strait without a compass.

I *can* read charts, to an extent. I would sit on my father's lap as he took wheelwatch at night, the red light over the captain's chair smoking the galley like a darkroom, keeping our eyes sharp for the outer lights of marker buoys and other vessels nearby. He would point out capes, shoals, dangers on the chart, and then the corresponding points on our radar or angles on our compass heading. I would nestle my face into the soft black rubber collar around the radar screen, staring into the black space and its green blips as a bright green line spun slowly around the circle like a timer hand, lighting up anything that pinged back.

The charts themselves were a swarm and scramble of lines and numbers, a busy chatter overlaid atop a picture of the water's expanse. Like topography in reverse, the lines and shades told stories about depths and rocks and trenches, safe passageways and no-man's lands and other more esoteric ways to break up the immensity of the ocean. Sometimes the charts were wrong or outdated due to erosion or changes in tides. Then came the skipper's knowledge, my father's familiarity with this cape or that, knowing how far the tide had to be in before we could safely shoot a gap between two rocks or which sandbar to skirt that was invisible to the eye.

When we first got a depth sounder, we would all gather around it to marvel at the pictures of the ocean floor that bloomed across the screen. It felt like cheating, in a way, to be able to watch the bottom in real time, its densities and shapes spelled it out in different colors.

We learned to read the difference between a rock and a clot of kelp, to guess which clusters were seaweed and which were schools of fish lurking down below.

The addition of GPS was another intervention, bringing us farther from our immediate senses and our shared knowledge through more traditional forms of navigation. Instead, we could simply see our position represented in the abstract, anywhere on the planet. The satellite perspective brought the entire earth into focus, and in so doing, zoomed us out and away from the personal link we had in the moment—to the waves around us, the familiar depths, the firsthand sense of place. Yet in other ways, it helped us see the connections between things, that wide perspective also a way of shrinking the infinite, showing us what really lay beyond the horizon.

"Lara, c'mere!" boomed my father's voice over the intercom on deck. I scrambled up the ladder to the flying bridge and entered the wheelhouse to find him playing with the new GPS.

"Here we are," he pointed, indicating the familiar outline of Kodiak Island on the screen. He zoomed out until the display showed little more than open water and pushed the key that would scroll us southward. Down, down, down—nothing but ocean expanse. For nearly a minute he scrolled, and I looked at his face to see what exactly it was I was supposed to notice.

He was smiling.

"There!" he said. Another island had come into view, a much smaller one—a cluster of islands.

"Where . . . ?"

"It's Hawaii," he beamed. "We could turn this puppy due south, and if we had enough fuel, we'd run smack-dab into paradise."

I looked southward out over the water, and the infinite no longer felt quite the same.

~

Traditional Hawaiian navigation, like most of Polynesia, relied upon complex knowledge of the stars and an ongoing calculus in the mind of the navigator based on relative speed and distance traveled. It required incredible memorization and awareness, but these wayfinding techniques—mental star compasses, cloud formations, tracking the flight paths of birds—were so accurate and successful that Polynesian seafarers were able to establish consistent trade routes that extended from New Zealand to South America in double-hulled canoes. At one point, their territory spanned over six million square miles of islands and open ocean, making it one of the largest ethnic (if not political) empires in history.

Familiarity with the water itself was also essential to their understanding of position. "If you can read the ocean, you will never be lost," says Master Navigator Nainoa Thompson. Knowledge of the ocean swells and the patterns of currents were central to their wayfinding for daylight travel and other times when the stars were not visible. Some neighboring groups, like the Marshallese, used wave-piloting almost exclusively and were able to navigate expansive and intricate atoll systems out of sight of land solely through sensitivity to the movement of the waves.

Unlike most of the other navigational systems of Oceania, the Marshallese did not use dead reckoning, the process by which one's position is determined in relation to a previous point or fix. In other words, they did not think about where they had come from and then construct a mental map of where they were heading. Instead, they focused on knowing where they were at any given moment in relation to the major ocean swells. In the same way that some navigators use the consistent position of a star or a prevailing wind, the Marshallese recognized consistent swells coming from the four cardinal directions, with *dilep*, or the eastern swell, being the strongest. Intersections between major swells formed nodes, and these nodes formed lines or paths through the water that could be followed with great consistency if one knew how to feel them. Rather than relying on mental images of the territory around them, they felt the movement of their craft and were able to detect complex patterns in the waves based on knowledge of the ways in which these cardinal swells were disrupted by land, regardless of whether the land was visible. This was based on a profound understanding of the ways in which water moves and how rocks and landforms influence underwater currents and wave patterns.

"Now I've heard some say wave bend around an island. Alright, I want to tell you right away that is not true," says Rongelapese navigator Lepedpedin. "No swell of this world know how to bend. They just roll in one direction and keep going."

Marshallese navigators could feel the changes in this roll to locate distant objects in the water. It was through this "remote sensing" of islands and other landforms that they moved through their atoll systems and beyond. In this way, the wayfinder was a bit like a spider in the center of a vast web, attuned to subtle tremors and changes in their environment in all directions.

Having such a simplified "navigational toolkit," one relying solely on waves, required an intense sense of presence and attention on the part of the navigator. Ocean travel was a completely immersive experience. To lose track of one's position could mean total disorientation, and without the accrued cues and awareness of the voyage, it was easy to make errors. On the other hand, there were currents and markers to help guide the voyager back on track as well. Navigators learned to trace the *okar*, or "root," an invisible line formed by a series of *booj*, or "knots," which are intersections of major swells as disrupted by a landform. "As the root, if you follow it, leads to the palm tree, so does this lead to the island," said one master navigator.

This way of knowing the waves, of seeing forces that are invisible to the eye, represents an entirely different form of understanding from the charts and equipment that cluttered our wheelhouse in

Alaska. It was an experiential form of knowledge in which the cognitive structures are of actions and tendencies, ways of interpreting shifting conditions in the moment rather than mental maps of places or things. The success of the navigation depended upon complete submersion within the experience, with only patterns as abstractions instead of projections or representations as with charts, or even directions, as with celestial navigation. Like the Inuit, Marshallese wayfinders had to be deeply present, attuned to both the gross movements of the swell as well as the tiny disruptions within it, feeling the movement of the water with staggering complexity, while also being in flow with their constantly changing conditions and relative position.

Unlike the Norse, the Marshallese had few names for the types of waves they encountered. In fact, when anthropologists and mariners sought out master wave-pilots, seeking to record their systems and knowledge for posterity—particularly post World War II, when the techniques fell rapidly into obscurity—the informants struggled to share what they knew simply because they lacked the language to do so. They had no words to describe the intimate knowledge they held in their sense of balance, their sensitivities to movement and rhythm, the patterns they knew intuitively and could trace but could not verbalize.

Even among the Marshallese themselves, handing down the knowledge of their wayfinding was a complicated and individualized process. Most used what have come to be called *stick charts*, elaborate and often beautiful two-dimensional structures crafted of palm fronds or pandanus root bound by coconut fibers. The most basic teaching tools were known as *mattang* charts, square cross shapes with symmetrical curves, like wicker mandalas. Mattang were not maps of places but rather representations of the ways in which the eastern swell and western swell would meet. The curves demonstrated the tendencies of currents and counter-currents within the swells; they noted the ways in which land and wind would change those fluid motions. They also noted disruptive wave patterns, or *lutokḷo, kkan*, meaning "pouring out and away from you," or trickster swells that could lead an unfocused navigator astray.

The mattang appear, to my untrained eye, both surprisingly simple and also esoteric, the symbolic shapes of intersection blooming from the center of the charts in intricate but balanced lines that recall both snowflakes and flowers, a reminder of the many similarities of geometry in natural forms, their graceful common mathematics.

Other types of charts included the *meddo*, which represented the unique wave and swell patterns specific to a given region. These charts were less symmetrical, more representative of physical space, with shells used to mark actual landforms—though relative distance and "true" position of the islands were neither needed nor incorporated into their navigational systems. Larger, more complex charts called *rebbelib* were made to represent entire island systems and their respective swell patterns. They were studied prior to voyages but not brought along on the trip itself, again, as reckoning from point to point was not part of their method.

While each type of chart was used by all navigators, the charts themselves further represent the individual, experiential aspect of their wayfinding knowledge: one chart could not be read by another navigator; in other words, each stick chart was made by the person who intended to use it and so served as a private mnemonic device rather than a map. The knowledge that was passed along was *how* to find one's way but not where or what that way may be.

Around World War II, the Japanese and Germans entered the region, and canoe travel between the islands was banned by colonial rule. Interest in contemporary, mechanized navigation quickly supplanted the memorization- and skill-intensive traditional methods, and by the time the United States conducted its nuclear weapons tests, detonating sixty-seven nuclear bombs on Bikini and Enewetak Atolls at the end of the war, Marshallese wayfinding had all but died out as local residents were forced to evacuate their homeland due to radiation poisoning, contaminated resources, and mandatory relocation. Once Rongelap Atoll was pronounced livable in 1957, a number of people returned, hoping to relearn their traditional means of navigation outside of colonial rule. Joseph Genz (2016) writes of the experiences of Captain Korent, a Marshallese navigator who participated in the revival of the tradition:

> He lay blindfolded in a canoe while his grandfather towed him to various positions around a coral islet so that he could determine his location based on how the intersections and reflections of incoming waves from the ocean and lagoon affected the motion of the canoe. Since Rongelap remained radioactive, however, this was a fleeting exercise in what would have under normal circumstances been numerous years of rigorous training.

Captain Korent's training was successful, however, and his work has continued to restore practices that have returned heritage and ways of knowing to his people. It is a difficult thing to recover, this kind of experiential knowledge, and one so deeply rooted in the pragmatic aspects of daily life—inter-island travel, once transformed, becomes a representation of different needs and a mode for new types of exchange within the evolving society. The culture cannot return to a time when other forms of navigation have not entered their consciousness, but it can seek to reclaim the intimacy it once had with the place in which it resides, one surrounded by waves for which they have no words.

As they restore their practices, they use the old terms for those things they do name: *kāāj in rōjep*, or "fishhook," is a wave formation to the northeast or southeast of an island; *nit in kōt* is a sign to the west, literally, "a pit where birds fight." *Reḷọk* is a misleading swell pattern, meaning "this will plunge you into the sea." They name the currents that lead away, as well: the first zone is called *jukae*, or "going into"; the second zone is *rubukae*, or "crossing"; the third zone is *jeljeltae*, when the signs become weakest, meaning "loosening," or "unraveling," as if the web and its tremors were coming undone. They also have a name for the fear the navigator feels when they lose the way altogether. They see it as a madness, the overwhelming sense of panic that comes when confronted with the vastness, when the patterns fall apart. They call it *wiwijet*, "the loss of direction," from which there is no coming home.

I know this feeling, this madness. Though I was only navigating the depths in my mind, it is this panic that overwhelmed me as a child, this contact with something far greater than I could understand. It was as if my tiny self were being set adrift in a space too big for knowing, too wild for naming. The intimate turns into terror—this is the nature of terrible awe.

5

Winch

I USED TO BE FEARLESS. Or maybe it's just that my parents raised me fearlessly. It was a different time, as they say—in the 1970s, people put their pot roasts in the oven inside plastic bags, playground slides had rust holes, and kids walked to school by themselves. No one I knew had ever heard of a bicycle helmet. To be young meant to be unsupervised, free to find risks and decide which to take.

My folks took it even a step further. Nomads at heart, they piled me onto motorcycles and into the beltless backs of pickup trucks. I flew, unaccompanied, on airplanes. I regularly talked to strangers. I fell from trees. My parents yanked me out of school whenever it suited their mood, knowing I could catch up on my own whenever I wanted, and knowing, too, that real learning happens outside the classroom. They drove me around the continental United States looking for new haunts, new hunting grounds, a new home.

By the time I was seven years old, I had been to all fifty states, though much of my experience was limited to what I could glimpse through the car window, peering my nose over the edge of the door, gnawing the soft pleather as the telephone poles stuttered past like a one-way metronome. We slept in seedy motels that smelled of curry and cigarettes, where a quarter would make the bed shake. Rather than paying for a cot, my folks just pulled out a drawer on the dresser and tumbled me in atop our laundry and those thin mesh blankets that are more holes than heat—at least, until I grew too long, which was sooner than they'd budgeted for.

Most fearlessly of all, they took me on the boat. When I was born, my mom kept me home on dry land for the first year, but once I turned two, I became part of the crew. Granted, I toddled around in a little orange life vest twenty-four hours a day—though this, too, probably contributed to my overall sense of invulnerability: I bounced like a rubber ball off all the sharp corners and hot surfaces of the galley, where I spent my days barricaded as the grown-ups worked on deck.

Now, a galley is hardly a playpen. There are knives, trapdoors to the engine room, and drawers full of gear. Everything is constantly shifting about, sliding and heaving with the swell. Not to mention the incredibly enticing—yet forbidden—panel of switches and toggles and small red lights that beckoned from the wall beside the captain's chair. My parents did a wonderful job casting their stern spell of prohibition on that panel—just walking past it sends shivers of anxiety through me even as an adult, lest I inadvertently brush against the lazarette switch or accidentally activate the bilge pump. Though really, a flipped switch may have been the least of their worries.

If you have spent time around piers and docks, then you know that most of those structures are fixed—in other words, they do not rise and fall with the tides. This means that, when one's boat is tied up to the dock and the water is high, getting onto the dock can be as simple as stepping from the bulwark to the boardwalk, sometimes even stepping *down*. But if the tide is low, and this can sometimes be really, really low, the pilings all stand naked and shivering in their tar, their skirts of mussels and barnacles glistening with the rainbow sheen of fuel that the scattered dish soap failed to disperse. That means a long climb up a very slimy ladder that spends half of its time submerged.

If you've ever had to carry gear, or groceries, or anything at all up a ladder, then you know the move it takes: the inchworm grab where you hug your body in close to the rungs, pull your feet up a step, balancing whatever you're carrying on a hip or a shoulder, and then undulate your whole body out and up, letting go completely for a fraction of a second as you whip your arm up a rung and pray to the gods of physics that you didn't get your balance wrong. Now imagine doing this with a shrieking toddler close to naptime in one arm, or with a young child lacking the wingspan to make the ascent on her own, whose ability to cooperate with the process may not quite make up for her shifting weight.

Away from port, the risks doubled. Much in the way I imagine other childhoods involved fears of the abandoned house at the end of their block, or the big old tree that had a crying face in the evening light, or the wordless school bus driver whose vocabulary of scowls kept all the kids in line, so did the various pieces of equipment on deck each take on auras of danger for me and stories to match.

Beware of the winch, my child, for get one finger caught in its clutches and your whole little body will snap in half before anyone knows what's happened. Don't touch the hydraulics, little one—or your mother could get dragged up to the block. Beware the towline, girl—it's really a whip in disguise that could take off your head. Watch the coils, kid—if your foot gets caught in a bight when the line goes out, it will take you with it. How well do you know how to swim?

And then there was the Troub-hole. The Troub-hole, or "trouble hole" was a cubby at the fore of the bunks, where we kept flotation suits and other emergency gear. For me, it was also my closet full of monsters, my bridge lurked by trolls. Fo'c'sle sounded like "folks' hole," sounded like "fox hole," like a dirt pit full of animals. I never actually got sent to the Troub-hole, but it lived in my world like a malevolent spirit, waiting to swallow me into its dark maw at the foot of the crew bunks. Any bad behavior met with the threat of exile to the Troub-hole, which was, of course, the only suitable place for naughty children to sit and think about their wrongdoings, like a portal to a realm of damp, black purgatory.

But like all childhood terrors, each held in its heart a kernel of delight. Standing near the winch, with its droning vibration as it tirelessly drew in the purse line, I thrilled to the image of getting trapped and whipped around its axis like a coyote in a cartoon. Every coil of line was like a challenge to step inside its snare: do you dare?

Do you dare?

I realize now, though, that the real fear must have been my parents'. They did what they had to do to make a living and, from day one, treated me like the tiny adult I thought I was. The Venn diagram of parenting and fishing looked like a perfect circle to them, one big enough to hold our family inside. They must have had their doubts about having a child on a boat, though—I know they did. Sooner or later, they'll tell you; if you spend any amount of time with my folks, you will inevitably hear a story about the Troub-hole.

"One evening, we were traveling around the island to get into position for an early-morning opener on the west side," my dad always begins, leaning back in his chair to assume his storytelling pose.

"Steph came racing up topside where I was on wheelwatch, and said, '*Is Lara with you?*'" He moans, waving his arms in a caricature of a hysterical mother.

My father touches his chest to show how his heart had stopped and turned to ice beneath his beard. He kills an imaginary throttle, bringing the boat to a slow standstill, tossing in its own wake.

He leans forward, gesturing with the toothpick that always miraculously appears from behind his ear when he wants to put a finer point on things.

"I knew that she would never ask if she hadn't already searched everywhere down below—as if there are so many places for a three-year-old to be on a forty-eight-foot fishing boat. The crew dropped the gear work they were sewing; we tore that cabin apart, flipping seat cushions and opening cupboards, we looked in the head, the engine room, even the fish hold."

He hangs his head for a dramatic pause. At this point in the telling, my mother's face draws in, pinched against the memory. She usually shakes her head.

"She'd gone overboard," my dad concludes. "We knew it. And we'd been traveling, so god knows when she'd disappeared. Hell, her body could have been anywhere for miles, if it hadn't sunk. It could have been anywhere." Here he says, "her body," I notice—putting distance between himself and the alternate little me that drowned.

He waits. My mother frowns and sighs heavily, her gentle scold against his words.

"'Tee hee hee!'" We froze. And then we waited for what felt like forever, and then from out of the Troub-hole, we heard it again:

"'Tee hee hee!'" He covers his mouth and rocks his shoulders like an imp.

"This little shit had crawled up in there, thinking she was so god-damned smart . . . I tell ya—years, we lost *years* off our lives in that one instant. Whoo!"

My mother nods.

I had apparently decided to engage in some self-administered immersion therapy and hide myself in the very place I was likely to get sent if I ever pulled that shit again. I remember that my parents pulled me from the dank cabinet and held me tight. Of course, I didn't understand what all the fuss was about, and as the crew ruffled my hair and kissed my head with rough beards and red eyes, I mar-veled at exactly *how much better I was than the adults* at hide-and-seek.

～

I have a child now, a beautiful nonbinary wildling, raised on land. When they were three, I was struck by the realization that, if our upbringings were the same, they would have been on the boat a for a year already. The thought of it made me sick to my stomach. At that age, they could barely cross the street without tearing from my hand and scampering across at their own pace. My heart leapt and sunk like a snagged corkline in my chest every time we navigated a parking lot. How could I have had them on a boat?

Before I was pregnant, a friend of mine told me that, once his children were born, he was never again without a seed of fear in his chest. At the time, I offered some naïve platitudes about how you can't hang on to them forever, or some such nonsense. I didn't yet realize what it is to love a thing so much more than oneself. I didn't yet know what it is like to gain something so great that holding it is its own kind of terror, because its very existence carries within it the shape of its loss.

Like most new parents, when my child was only a baby, I used to slink into their bedroom just to listen to their breath moving in and out of their lungs, to reassure myself that their chest was, indeed, still rising and falling just as it should. But as the specter of SIDS faded when they passed the year mark, and then the second year, I found that the anxiety never completely went away. Even now, on the rare occasion when they fall asleep in the car, I have to resist the urge to shake their growing knees and wake them up, just to know that they haven't simply left this world as abruptly and magically as they entered it.

The mystery is too much for me—the fact that they exist, that they are real. I miscarried once before they were born. I was thirty-four, not old by today's standards, but historically speaking, downright geriatric for a first-time mother, and as the bleeding began and the future I had so longed and planned for dissolved in tears, I told myself that my body simply couldn't do it. After years of anxious birth control, the great irony of my life would be barrenness. I had waited too long. And so, when I did conceive again, when my pregnancy went to term, when all signs indicated a thriving, healthy baby, I still didn't allow myself to believe that it could happen, not entirely.

Complications during their birth nearly proved my fears true—a tangled cord, a slowing heart; I was sure I couldn't do it right. It wasn't until I held them in my arms, a screaming, sticky, angry, mottled little gorgeous fuzzy squirm of reality, that I was able to accept that this was something I could do, that I could *have*. And ever since that moment, just as my friend said, I carry not only that searing wonder that they have all their parts and they keep working with or without my urging them on, without my own body as life support, but also the shadow of how tenuous and unlikely their existence seems. I am haunted by the fear of its loss. It is as if I arrived in the present moment only by the slimmest breath of a chance—if I think too hard on it, some prior step or choice may slip, rewrite itself, and I will find myself in another life altogether, one without them.

My child is not particularly reckless, though they do get the devil's gleam in their eyes sometimes. They don't like to be alone. They still like to be held before bed. They are afraid of getting their hands sticky, of being looked at by crowds of people, of being licked by dogs. They would never hide in a Troub-hole. When they want to climb trees, I let them. When they want to clamber over rocks, I watch and cheer them on.

My dad occasionally wonders aloud if they did the right thing, raising me like they did. "We knew you never had a chance to be normal," he says, thinking perhaps of the summers I never spent on Slip 'N Slides, or eating marshmallows at summer camps. "I always regretted that," he sometimes adds.

I don't regret it at all.

That was a gift that was given to me by my parents: they took risks and showed me how to manage them; they trusted me with mistakes. Their courage—or maybe folly—allowed me to step into the world with curiosity and even recklessness, and though it didn't always keep me safe, it did help me be strong in the times that I wasn't.

My greatest fear now is that I will not be able to offer the same to my child, that our landlocked urban life will hold the wrong kinds of peril—drunk drivers, drugs, boredom. There are no winches in our tiny house in the middle of the big city. We don't go to sleep hearing the waves slap against the hull, promising dreams of drowning in the abyss. I fear my own rough adventures are behind me, that I will fail to set the kind of example for them that I had, that they will lack the opportunity to test themself against the raw edges of the natural world. I fear my child will not grow up fearless enough, a tiny pioneer in a frontier all their own. I want to teach them to run into the world, to be wild *and* wise. I want them to know that the risks can set them free.

6

Buoy

bu·oy /ˈbo͞oē/ *n.* 1. an anchored float serving as a navigation mark, to show reefs or other hazards, or for mooring. 2. a rubber flotation device used as cushion between a vessel and another surface. *v.* 3. keep (someone or something) afloat.

July 22, 1981

MY MOM CALLS SCOTTIE A GORILLA. I think it's because he's so hairy when he struts around deck with his shirt off, but he also smells really bad, so it could be that too. I don't mind—he's my favorite deckhand. It's my fifth birthday, and he promised to help me jig for cod. We get a fat spool of white twine and a wicked hook the size of my hand, and he ties it on the end for me. My dad brings me some chicken livers to use for bait. He slathers some peanut butter on them, and we jam them on the hook and plop it down into the water. I let it sink, feeding the line out between my hands until I feel the slight slack that tells me it's hit the bottom. Dad says cod'll eat almost anything—but they especially like peanut butter.

I stand there at the side of the boat in my life vest and jig. All I have to do is jerk my hand every once in a while to make it look like the bait is moving. I jig, and then wait a long moment, then jig again. I catch myself counting to fill in the spaces and try to make them random, so my birthday cod down there will think the bait is alive. My hand gets tired, so I tie the line off on a cleat and then drag a buoy over to the edge of the boat. It's fat and pink and half my size and has our call number inked onto the side. I untie my line and sit on the buoy, bouncing, jigging. Scottie comes to check on me.

"Catch anything yet?" He smiles, and I hear the grown-ups laughing in the galley. My stomach feels hot and twisty, embarrassed. I briefly wonder if there aren't really any cod down there, but I'm determined to get a fish. Maybe my mom will fix it for supper—we can cook it on the hibachi on deck, like when we caught the octopus and it tried to climb out of the pot on the stove, so we grilled its tentacles piece by piece instead.

Mom is baking a cake inside. I can smell the chocolate from the little stove inside the galley. She's been hiding the frosting ingredients and the box in the cubby under her bunk. I know she has presents, too, but I can't figure out where she hides those. When I catch this cod, we'll have a real party, with cake and presents. Maybe we'll even get to tie up next to another boat tonight, and there will be music, and everyone will be happy.

I feel a tug. I yank back against it, the way I've been taught. You have to set the hook into the fish's mouth, which sounds to me like it would hurt, but the grown-ups say that fish don't feel. The line starts to run out between my hands, and it feels like I'm holding fire. I scream for help and kick the buoy out of the way. My dad rushes onto the deck and is beside me before I can drop the line.

"Pull it in!" he shouts. "You got one!"

I wrap the line around one hand and pull and pull, but it's too strong for me. I hear my mom yelling from the galley not to let me go overboard. My dad puts one big hand on the line, and Scottie appears at my elbow and puts his gorilla hand on there, too, and we're all pulling and pulling until the huge ugly face of a cod comes out of the water. He's angry and splashing, but I'm jumping up and down because I did it.

"I caught him!" I squeal. My dad is laughing and patting me on the back, and Scottie helps me haul it on deck. "We can have it for dinner!" I yell. My chest feels like it's going to burst the bindings on my vest.

My dad gets a fillet knife, the mean-looking one that curves, and he cuts the fish open there on the hatch covers, slicing up its belly toward its head. He pulls the fish open, and the entire inside of its body is covered in tiny white ringlets. A few of the ringlets twitch and squirm, and I realize that the cod is riddled with worms. I look up at my dad.

"Most cod have worms," he shrugs, matter-of-factly. "Sorry, kiddo." He tosses the carcass back overboard and I watch the water close darkly over my fish as it sinks out of sight.

July 22, 1983

I awake in my bunk before the rest of the crew, drawing my legs quietly from my sleeping bag as if shedding a fat skin. I tiptoe out of the dank cave of snores and grunts that is the fo'c'sle and up into the galley. My bare feet make no sound on the linoleum, my weight insufficient to creak in even the trapdoor in the floor that leads to the engine room. The stateroom door is closed; my parents are sleeping, too—though the early morning light is already flooding lemon through the top half of the split steel door leading to the deck. I thrill at this rarest of moments: I am all by myself. I climb the single step up to the door, the step that serves double duty as a gear cubby. *Bequietbequietbequiet*, I think. It squeaks. I freeze. A pause, and the snores continue. I carefully unclick the thick steel handle and escape onto the deck.

I am intensely *awake*. The surface of the deck is rough beneath my feet, painted dark gray and covered in grit that keeps our boots from slipping in the wet. My senses crackle. I take a deep breath. Already I hear the clangs and toots and mechanical exhalations from the cannery processing fish; forklifts buzz on the boardwalk overhead. It is low tide, and our boat sits far below the dock, rocking gently against the tarred pilings on an invisible wake. Lines creak in the rigging above me. The buoys rub against the side, protesting softly with rubber balloon voices.

Though I know no one can hear me now, I still tiptoe, easing onto the rise of the hatch covers that seal the fish hold in the center of the hull. The skiff is cinched up behind the stern, the towline taut, drawing a straight line from the rear bulwark to the winch at the front of the deck. I trace the cold metal chevrons in the hatch covers with a toe and sit on the towline. It bows a bit beneath me but holds fast. No one is there to yell at me for sitting on a line under pressure. The skiff creaks, and I hear the slop of wavelets against the hull. Other boats are lined up against the pilings of the dock, still sleeping, their windows dark. I feel preternaturally aware, as if I were peering into the world and seeing through to the other side.

I am, for this moment, a ruler of a vast and strange domain, one completely without adults. I am overwhelmed, for an instant, by the very *now*ness of it all, and I remember: today is my birthday. I take yet another deep breath and exhale it, wondering aloud, "I am *seven*." I feel impressively old.

Eventually, the rest of the crew wakes up and my reign evaporates. I am small and lost underfoot in the bustle of boat work. My main job is staying out of the way and not falling overboard; two things I am very good at. I draw pictures of fish and other sea creatures and read books written for grown-ups because that's what there is to read. Right now, I'm most of the way finished with *Gone with the Wind*.

After breakfast, Scottie presents me with a small package wrapped in newspaper. I unwrap it and find a little box. Inside is a red soapstone salmon with fins that stick out and tiny gills and eyes carved in white. He made it with a pocketknife in stolen moments over the past few weeks. I throw my arms around his neck and give him a big hug. He gorilla hugs me back. "Now don't you lose that," he warns. "That salmon's good luck. It's going to make us a lot of money." He winks, and I promise to keep it forever.

Later, Mike, a deckhand from another boat, shouts down from the dock. The tide is coming in, and he doesn't have far to shout. I love the scratchiness of his voice; he always sounds like he just woke up. He hops down the ladder and sits beside me on the net, shyly offering me a coloring book and some crayons. "Happy birthday, Lara Lee," he says, and ruffles my hair. I lean into him and say thank you. Being the only girl in the fleet means I have a hundred big brothers. They all miss their own sisters or daughters back home, and they treat me like their own.

Next comes Joe, who, as far as I know, is a famous gambler. He brings me two decks of cards from a casino in Vegas and two dollars to play the slots. By late afternoon, I've received two flashlights with batteries, four hand-drawn cards, one batch of cookies, some Norwegian money ("To buy yourself a candy bar when you visit me in Oslo"), and three copies of the same coloring book, since it's the only one for sale at the cannery store. They're all apologetic for their gifts, and bashful. They all have the same comforting reek of saltwater jeans and beards. The smell of halibut frying in saltine crusts keeps them hanging near the cabin, and before long, music is coming through the speakers on deck, and everyone is sitting around in their rubber boots, eating off paper plates and talking and drinking beer from cans.

My dad hauls a buoy down from up topside and works a thick snap through the hole on top where the buoy line is knotted through. I clap my hands excitedly, guessing what comes next. He clips the snap to the line going over the block and to the other overhead winch, so he can pull the buoy both upward and side to side with the hydraulics, the way we swing the brailer when we deliver fish. He grins at me. "Wanna get on?"

I climb onto the buoy and wrap my legs around tight, gripping the line like a barnacle, terrified and thrilled in equal measure. My dad grabs the rope still dangling from the buoy and gives it a tug, sending me swinging back and forth across the deck, toward the stern and then back toward the cabin. He zings me upward so the buoy misses the deck winch, and then lets it out as I arc away again. I can't stop grinning. "HIGHER!" I shriek.

With every pass, I see a blur of faces, laughing. I see flickers of flannel shirts and long hair. I zoom through clouds of smoke—from the grill, from cigarettes, from joints being passed around—and whirl away again, now spinning dizzily over the swirl of the net, now careening wildly close to the rigging. Sometimes someone will stagger in my path and we'll collide, and I'll hang on and they'll tumble onto the deck. I am flying, eye to eye with a passing seagull, then wheeling downward, tucking into a tight spin and stretching out to slow myself. Once my dad tries to make my stomach lurch by dropping the line quickly from the block, but I fall too fast and the buoy bumps on the web, instead, and I roll off onto the cork pile, laughing so hard I can't breathe.

The party continues to swirl: *everyone* is laughing now, high and crazy. I'm drinking orange soda from a can, and half the faces on deck are ones I don't even recognize. There was a cake, and all of that has been eaten too. Men are whooping and the sky is the bright pale of July evenings, and someone else is on the buoy, someone else at the controls. He flies well past the edge of the boat, and there is a breathless instant when we all watch, and yes, he loses his grip right at that instant, and there is a colossal splash and then someone gets a hook to haul him out of the water, and the laughter is more like a roar, a wild sound just on the fringe of control. A fight has broken out on another boat nearby, and drunken voices are shouting. Nobody watches. I find my mom's face in the crowd on deck and she is smiling, her hair down and loose over her shoulders. These are my favorite times—when no one is working, and no one near me is mad, and everybody, everybody plays.

July 22, 1988

The rumble of the engine makes a heavy, relentless vibration in the walls and deck of the boat, even up topside. The buzzing grind of it matches my mood as I crouch in the corner, seething behind a pile of buoys near the chest freezer. We were supposed to go back to Oregon last week for a break. I was going to have a normal birthday—one with people my own age, with my friends from school. I was going to have a party and do normal things like go swimming or roller skating or whatever regular kids do. I wasn't going to be pitching fish and hanging out with my parents and the rest of the crew. Again. But then the runs got hot, and we couldn't afford to take the time off, to miss the fish.

Who gives a shit about fish? I'm a *kid*. At twelve years old, I'm convinced I should have some kid time, for chrissake. It's not like we hang out in the cannery anymore, anyway—it's just fishing and more fishing, and when we're not fishing, we're mending gear. Nobody has parties anymore; nobody rafts up in the evenings for barbecues or goes beachcombing in the small bays after delivering their fish. I hate it. I want a normal summer with camp and suntans and popsicles like in the movies.

I press the back of my head against the railing behind me as hard as I can, and the engine vibration slowly turns me to goo—the relaxation runs down my body and through my spine and into my palms, where the only sensation left is the grit of the topside deck.

The buoys form a protective fort around me, an igloo made of spheres. They are huge and orange-pink; it's like being nestled in a giant salmon redd full of glowing fish eggs. They are warm as skin from sunlight and the heat from the stack nearby, exhaling their comforting rubber smell, mixed with diesel smoke and the ubiquitous tang of seawater. I rub a finger against the rounded surface of one closest to my face and trace off a fine line of salt left behind from the sun. It leaves a thin sparkle on my fingertip. A breeze tousles my hair and I tilt my face back to the sun. All I can see is buoy pink and jagged pieces of loud blue above, flares of light against my eyelids. This is my tree house, my summer secret space. The smell of lemon cake dances up from the galley window below: my mom's peace offering to me.

I enjoy a last few minutes before I am found. I decide I have made a big enough scene that my absence will have been noticed. There is always work to be done, and nowhere can one get away. I hide in my round pink-orange nest for a few minutes longer and then screw my angry face back on, climb out, and stretch. I slink down the ladder to the deck, jumping down the last two rungs, and look for something that needs done.

July 22, 1994

We slide up alongside the tender like a raiding party, quiet and dark. The huge boat looms over our smaller one, all mechanical noise and blaring white deck lights, the contrast turning a purple twilight into dense black. The pumps are running full blast, sucking out the hold of another boat on the other side. The other deckhand and I toss our buoys over the side and stand ready to catch the tie-up lines from the tender crew, slipping them quickly through the scuppers and tying off on the cleats as we gently scooch parallel to her hull. I smile up into the rigging and admire the shape of her, the heavy lines and thick build of the cabin. It's always a treat to deliver to the F/V *Balaena*. She has a soft-serve ice cream machine on board and a state-of-the-art fish pump, so offloading is fast and furious. Plus, her crew works like their asses are on fire, so we're usually in and out as quickly as possible, which means dinner sooner and more rack time for all of us.

Tonight, I don't even care. Tonight, I don't have to pitch or sort at all—it's my birthday. My birthday present from my dad is that I get to slip away and go for a soak while the boys take care of the delivery. Nothing could be more coveted, and I know the other deckhands think I'm spoiled because my father is the skipper. Let them think it. Within minutes I'm leaping from our deck to the other, clean dry clothes and a towel in hand.

The best part of the *Balaena*, besides the fact that my friend Shawn is the deck boss, is that past the engine room, around the corner, and through a poorly marked side hatch, is a small room that contains nothing more than a wooden bench and a saltwater hot tub, big enough for one.

The light inside the room is siren red, and between the light and the valves and open pipe-work everywhere, it gives the tub the feel of

being in a Soviet submarine, except for the luxury. This is the great
irony of being on a boat: one's life is spent surrounded by water, but
it is the rarest of things to be submerged—and warm. I shove off
my boots and peel off my socks and sweatpants, all half-soaked and
crusted on the edges with salt and fish gurry. My shirts and under-
clothes come next, and I marvel at how quickly a thing becomes
untouchable: what was once comfortably next to my skin now seems
utterly disgusting and corrupt. I can barely stand to drop it into a
pile beside my boots, let alone imagine wearing it on my body.

I step into the water with a hiss that echoes against the walls of
the small chamber. The sound of my voice is loud, even with the
underclang of the engine and the deck noise seeping dimly through
the walls. It is *hot*, and I feel my skin tighten as if trying to escape my
frame. I ease myself down into the tub until the water reaches my
chin and feel my skin prickle in protest, first burning, then freezing,
then melting into an exhale as my muscles slowly unlock their million kinks and edges.

It takes me a long time to find all the places where the tension still holds me together—my shoulders remain as tight as two
wooden blocks; my ass attempts to hover off the floor of the tub. It
is minutes before I realize my jaw is clenched. I lean my head against
the wall and exhale as slowly as I can, letting the rhythmic pattern of
the engine count for me in a rapid cycle, its mechanical pulse familiar and soothing, like the growl of a vast animal protector.

How many minutes do I have? I try to guess. Eight? Maybe
twelve? For these few minutes, I am buoyant, weightless. I get to drift
in a body I can barely feel. I get to be almost clean. Even showers are
a rarity on boats, and they are never as soothing as one would hope.
Marine showers involve getting wet as quickly as possible, turning
off the water and soaping up in awkward cold, then rinsing off in a
matter of seconds. It is refreshing, rejuvenating, but water rationing
keeps it from ever being relaxing. This handful of minutes feels at
once limitless and agonizingly short. I stare into the red of the walls,

imagining I am inside an enormous body, listening to its cells, its systems and heartbeats. As if I were floating in a giant seawater womb.

I hear the hydraulics hauling the pump out of our hold and back to the deck of the tender, so know they are in the final clean-up phase. I haul myself out of the tub and dry off slowly, carefully pulling on clean, dry clothes, stepping gingerly onto the damp concrete beneath me as if I were somehow made delicate, as if I didn't spend my days hauling gear and sleeping in my filthy, sweat- and slime-stained clothes. I run a brush through my long hair and linger a moment longer, smelling the skin of my own arm, the salt water drying upon it, the animal smell of me that is both warm and so familiar. Then I wrap my dirty things in the newly wet towel and step back out into the splashing wet night, the flail of fish and diesel, feeling temporarily clean and reborn.

July 22, 1997

I spend my twenty-first birthday in a bar, but they've been letting me into Tony's since I was seventeen, so it doesn't feel like much of a rite of passage other than the fact that I don't have to pretend I forgot my ID. The interior is dim and noisy, as usual. I avoid the back corner, where the coke dealers sell single lines, and stay close to the bartender, who is the only other woman in the place. My friends are already half-cocked; Juan is getting ready for trouble, his hands tapping restlessly at the bar and his jokes are getting mean. Dean is drooping maudlin. He still has a black eye from the bar two nights ago. I am bored, absentmindedly stirring my Jack and Coke with its little straw.

There's a bad vibe in here tonight; the hair on the back of my neck is standing up, and I keep looking toward the doors, my glance snapping up whenever the voices get louder, anticipating a fight. I can feel the leers boring into me from all directions. I imagine myself encased in steel, like a statue of Jeanne d'Arc. The attention both heats me and makes me want to run. The entire fleet is in town with nothing to do—we've been on strike for a while, and there's no end to the standoff in sight. So not only are people not making money but they've run out of gear and boat work to keep them busy, and all that's left to pass the time is to drink or to fight. Bloody faces and broken windows are a nightly occurrence.

"Let's get out of here," I say, and the rest of my drink disappears in a single swallow.

We exit into the alley behind the bar, and three guys are there, smoking. "Hey Darlin'," one slurs in my direction. "Where do you think you're goin'?" I walk quickly, and my friends flank me, instinctively. Two men is not necessarily protection from these feral bastards, especially if someone happens to have a gun or a knife, but it's better than being alone.

It's clear to me how boredom is close to violence. Keep these men busy, and they're hard workers and focused. But when the prices are too low to fish and the association is blocking the harbor with boats and guns to keep folks from scabbing, everyone is right on the line of trouble.

We pass the Harbormaster's and make our way down to the ramp into the harbor. The sky is clear, and the moon is there, cold above the sodium lights. A sea lion barks somewhere in the shadows, and I remember that there is a law against shouting at them—for your own good. An angry sea lion will just drag you off the pier and hold you underwater till you quit kicking, I've heard.

Juan lights a cigarette, his silhouette briefly carved in flame before disappearing into the dark again. He doesn't believe in the strike, thinks we should be fishing even for the insulting scrap of change we're being offered by the canneries. He's just here for the money, he says. He doesn't give a shit about politics. I tell him he's a fucking idiot.

This is Juan's second year in Alaska. Dean's been here longer but not by much. They're both good deckhands, I'm sure. I don't know—

they're not on my boat, thank god. But they just came for the money, like he says. They don't plan on making this a life; hell, they may not make it the season. They don't have any idea what it used to be like.

We used to fish five days on and have two days off—to rest, to do gear work, to talk. We used to take the skiff and go beachcombing, or pick berries, or hunt. Boats would raft up together in the evenings sometimes, and folks would share food and play guitar. Then the openings and closures changed. Instead of five on, two off, we'd fish until Fish & Game said to stop, and sometimes it would be weeks before a closure, and then we could just go somewhere else and keep fishing. We never rafted up in the evenings. We stopped thinking of the rest of the fleet as friends, and instead formed small alliances, talking in code over the radio and painting our boats gray to hide in the fog.

Even with all this time off, I can't remember the last time we had a party that felt like fun. Everybody drinks to forget how angry they are, how broke, how bored.

The guys want to get high, but I'm not in the mood tonight. I say goodnight at their boat and make my way down to the other end of the pier, to the finger where my boat sits quietly, my name painted on the side. I pass a pile of buoys and hear a groan coming out from underneath it. I think about walking right on past, but the groan comes again, so I stop. I push a buoy aside with a toe and see a pair of legs sticking out. A dirty hand reaches out from under the pile and shoves another buoy aside, and I can just barely make out a shadow where a face might be.

"Hey." The voice is phlegmy, soaked in cheap wine.

"Hey," I say. "You OK?"

"Fuck you." I'm not even sure he is talking to me. I can hear in his voice that he is Native, and I think for the thousandth time about alcoholism and ancestry and loss. Most of my Native friends live in dry villages. The ones who live here in town have it rough in a differ-ent way. He stirs for a moment, and I think he is going to try to sit up, but after a brief struggle against gravity, he drops his hand. I can see the harbor lights reflecting in his eyes. He is definitely looking at me. He points a curled finger at what is no doubt my double image.

"You don't belong here," he croaks.

I walk back to my boat, thinking he is probably right.

July 22, 1979, is written on the back of the Polaroid.

There I sit, chopped bangs framing a face that is nothing but eyes. I'm swaddled in a red and orange life vest that rises up around my neck, making my shoulders look hunched. My dad is on one side, making sure I don't fall in. Scottie is on the other, pretending to push me. My legs are bare, my feet swinging over the fish hold, which is full of seawater. We are tanked down, and the salmon we've caught are still alive, swimming in silver tornadoes beneath my feet. I'm holding a fishing rod made of a stick and a piece of twine; there's likely no hook on the end, but I am happily dipping the string into the water, kicking my toes back and forth in the cold, delighted as the slick, solid bodies of fish brush past me. I look like there is nowhere in the world I'd rather be.

7

Number

THERE ARE 360 DEGREES OF LONGITUDE, slicing the world like an orange. There are only 180 degrees of latitude—you can only go so far north before you are going south again—but along the rotation of the Earth on its axis, the degrees roll past in an endless loop. Each degree can be sliced into 60 minutes, and each minute into 60 seconds. In this way, the earth is like a clock, ticking its slices as it turns relative to an imaginary pin stuck in space above the equator.

My brain loves this information, loves the sweet, mystical *ahh* of natural mathematics, the sense of the universe whispering a tiny secret. These secrets also open a back door straight to my more compulsive, obsessive mind.

Sometimes I feel this ticking, the slices, and the hidden part of my brain starts to chew these lines, sensing, not calculating, circumference and rotational speed. The invisible grid stretches out before me in a thick, bending net. When I'm on deck, moving over the water, I almost see the lines hiss across the surface like traveling snakes, describing smooth arcs. When I'm on the shore, the lines penetrate landforms and describe a perfect sphere beneath the bumps and valleys of the earth. The math is elegant, an exact fit to the fractal mess of the real world.

The turn of the numbers is a white noise, a background pulse, the jagged green biotelemetry beep. We'll be traveling, the boat carving a frothy scar across the skin of the waves, and a voice will whisper: one thousand twenty-three. Or a blue gleam behind my eyes will form: two thousand six hundred forty.

What? I'll think. *Where did that number come from?*

And then I'll realize—I've been counting. Counting what, exactly? I'm never sure if it's a real thing or an imagined one, wavelets on the surface of the water, pixels on a vast, magnetic screen. Counting corks as they toc off the stern, their rhythmic gallop the sound of work. Counting the number of times a shackle clinks with the swell. The number of times the other deckhand spits on the deck after I've washed it.

This is not a gift. I am no mathematical genius, intuiting the cartographic geometry that took centuries and clocks and countless paradigm shifts to even learn to calculate. I'm no Kim Peek, the Rain Man, counting the Sundays in a decade, or Bobby Fischer, finding lines that will conquer an opponent a dozen moves ahead. My brain finds patterns, but not in a useful way. My patterns are baroque and exhausting, the output of a mind with too much energy and no particular gifts to spend it on other than compulsions. The patterns demand exponential spirals that move in and back out, layers within layers when stacking the leads into a perfect, orderly loaf. For better or worse, our back deck was a fastidious wet dream of tidy, manicured net—every set a staging to sell your dream seiner, as long as it wasn't too windy or the set gone wrong, or piles of kelp and jellies hadn't fouled the lines. I would count throws of cork line or the leads, my arm span a perfect fathom, endlessly measuring and tossing, measuring and tossing, to the end of the lead line's 1725 feet.

Sometimes I counted something else. There is another tic, one much chewier and less abstract than longitude or loops. There is a special challenge for OCD brains, one that is invisible, I suspect, to the neurotypical—making one's way down the boardwalk.

The heavy lumber of the dock is weathered and tarred as old railroad ties, enormous nail heads protruding here and there where the wood has worn away or the pressure of the tides has pushed them upward. It's a veritable minefield for the weird and sensually sensitive. I always thought someone at the cannery should crawl the length of it, checking for up-sticking nails. That should have been my job. I would have found a mathematically gorgeous and deeply unnecessary zigzag as I went on hands and knees, my small iron sledge in hand to pound down snags. But for me, the hardest job is to finish the pattern my feet find and make it to the end of the goddamn dock.

As soon as I climb up the ladder from the boat, I step on the edge of a plank. The edge presses upward into the arch of my foot through my boot. The pressure on my arch triggers a sensation in my mouth, a tension and physical impatience not unlike needing to pee. Once this sensation begins, I have to balance that pressure on both feet, complete a particular sequence, and find a resolution to the pattern that emerges, what I call an *escape*, before I can make it subside. It's a bit like being haunted by a hungry ghost with a taste for geometry. Or maybe like trying to quit smoking if cigarettes were made out of math.

If I'm lucky it was my right foot that started, as my brain leans that way, and it's much easier to find resolution to a pattern if it starts and ends on the right. If the tic begins on the left, I could be there for a while.

Right foot—left foot. My eyes seek out the edges of planks to create the matching pressures on my arches. It's a lot to keep track of when you're walking, eyes down to find the right boards and lines— *step on a crack, break your mother's . . . wait*—but still head up and acting, you know, normal.

The pattern unspools in my mind's eye. Left foot—right. It makes an arch-like shape itself [*arch-arch*], in my head, a mix of uprights and laterals, moving up and over. Once the right foot sequence ends, I then have to do it on my left: left foot—right foot—right foot— left. Now an arch on the left.

But now the pattern opens. You can't just begin on the right and end on the left, because that, too, is only half of a sequence, an arch, so now I would need to do the whole thing in reverse: left foot— right foot—right foot—left, then right foot—left foot—left foot—

right again. This creates, what my brain calls, an *opening*. The pattern unspools like origami unfolding itself.

My mouth clicks.

I echo the pattern of my feet with my tongue, sucking at the teeth on one side and then the next, or clicking my palate with a horsey tic. Then I can have one pattern on the ground and another in the box of my head.

Soon, the layers build. As my feet tap out the structure, my tongue plays its counterpoints, sometimes coinciding with the arches the steps build, sometimes the opposite, or a beat or two off. Each variation adds another level to the sequence that I have to resolve and mirror on the other side. My brain tracks these levels by constructing a mental image of a tower of crystal sticks. Beautiful, transparent slivers of light gleam like ice in my mind's eye, a vast, helix chandelier written in echoes and rounds, growing larger and more densely complex with every iteration. Each arch adds a wall or series of sticks—so it is always clear to me what the next move needs to be. I don't need to remember it; I only have to watch and obey the intense demands of its tessellations. Sometimes the structure becomes so large I cannot see the entire thing at once as I walk. I only pay attention to the top tiers, as those are the ones that will, sooner or later, provide resolution—the *escape*.

Sometimes sounds come with it, like an orchestra swelling toward a final chord but never quite reaching it [*da-du-da-du-da-DUM*], one instrument or another always looping it back around to the near finish, delaying the climax [*dum-da-du-DUM!*]. Sometimes, between the stepping and the clicking and the ticking and horn section and the board creaks and the crescendos, it gets very loud.

Sometimes it is hard to hide it. I will leap from one board to another, an absurd choice of step for a neurotypical walker, but necessary for my pattern—crucial, in fact. Missing the pressure on my arch could mean having to start all over again, the crystal tower crashing down like a shower of glass toothpicks—or worse, it could miss the pressure and absorb that into the pattern, could add a new permutation, meaning everything that came before would repeat again, to incorporate the new addition and mirror it accordingly. I try not to look ridiculous, lunging and stuttering for the right boards. I learn to stay smooth and say nothing about it.

I do all this as I'm walking, carrying things to the laundry, talking with others.

"Hey—what's up?"

"Hey." (*lunge*)

"What are you doing?"

"Oh, just hitting mug up!" (*step-step-step*)

If I come to the end of the boardwalk before the pattern completes, I have a choice: I can turn around and walk back the way I came, which sometimes works and sometimes only starts a new loop; or I can hang the pattern in the back of my mind and return to it later. This leaves me with a nagging, desperate feeling that, as an adult, I have learned, is not unlike jonesing for the object of addiction. The need to complete the pattern is a fierce and demanding master.

And yet, circumstances don't always allow me to wander the docks, clicking my tongue and building crystalline math castles in my head. I can't always silently count the number of times my thumbs brush my index fingers in unison—clutching and releasing a symphony of muscles in mirrored response. The patterns are distracting and consuming. I learn to turn down the volume on the orchestra and let the crystals tinkle and crash around my shoulders. I practice making the urges smaller, able to be tucked away or hidden under other thoughts, other gestures. I fold them in to my speech. I swallow them. I try to ignore the urgency of the ticking, the clicking, the pressure in my feet and tongue. Sometimes I have to grit my teeth around the numbers in my mouth and just walk.

8

Knot

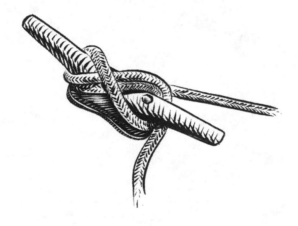

I WAS A WEIRD, AWKWARD GIRL at school in the Lower 48. I hated malls and pop music, preferring instead books with dragons on the covers and inventing small rituals in the woods around my home. Unlike note-folding, dance routines, or curling my bangs into a stiff-walled pouf, one of the few esoteric girlish practices I found myself capable of mastering was the art of tying friendship bracelets. Knotted patterns made sense to my clicky brain, and I loved watching their internal shapes reveal themselves through repetition. There were flat, woven bracelets with stripes and twisting, ropelike bracelets that resembled DNA, each individual knot cinching just a tiny bit shy of the last. In high school, other weird girls and I learned the ritual of spiraling these around slender braids in one another's hair. We attached small charms that made us jingle and glint and feel part of a very small, magical tribe.

This tiny secret witchcraft also prepared me for sailor's knots, for the summers when my landscape shifted from Oregon high desert to Alaska waters, where I traded the impenetrable drama of high school for the blunt company of fishermen. I was never quite strong enough, big enough, or boy enough to be treated like an equal on deck either. But unlike diesel mechanics, running a skiff, or talking shit about other crews' cork piles, the magic of knots was something from the man's world of fishing I knew I could do well.

Traditionally, sailors also used knots as magic. In many parts of the world, sorcerers, wizards, shamans, or witches would bind the wind in a cord or length of line. Sailors would purchase these knots and take them to sea as guarantees against doldrums. Wind knots were often sold in sets of three. Knot magic is a structural spell, so untying the knot releases the binding: undo one for a healthy breeze, two for a strong wind; three could unleash a gale.

The link between lines and storms is strong. Sailing culture forbade whistling because a whistler could be seen as challenging the wind, and anyone who'd witnessed a hurricane firsthand knew the wind would always win. The wind was seen as something twisting, something that could be coiled and spun, like rope and like thread. Spinning wheels were forbidden aboard ships because their motion was thought to have the power to summon a storm, as well. It is also possible that this was related to the taboo against allowing women on board, since spinning was considered "women's work." However, *naked* women were considered *good* luck, which is why they grace the bow of so many ships as figureheads, breasts typically bared to the spray. Apparently, exceptions could be made.

Knots themselves have a power to them that is magical—some knots break, and some simply don't. They are more than just puzzles; they are small wonders of physics and friction. Some are designed to seize and others to slip, and this truth has generated whole realms of exploration in both craft and science. What makes a knot strong? What makes it give? Why do some turn to stone under tension and others pop apart? Why are some so damn hard to untie?

The trick of undoing them requires a calm head and an eye for the place where the knot "cracks," the tension point that holds it in place. My mother has always been the best at this, an example of gentleness being the greatest form of strength. She resists the temptation to scream or overpower a tangle with macho force, patiently following an end back through the snarl until it falls apart in her lap at long last. While Alexander the Great skipped the puzzle of the Gordian Knot and simply hacked through it with his sword, the old sailor adage teaches that the best way to figure out how to untie a knot is to learn how to tie it in the first place.

The first complex knot I learned to tie was the fisherman's knot, or more poetically, the lovers' knot, wherein two opposing basic knots slide against one another and hold each other tight, more than doubling their strength. My mom showed me how one looped to the right over the opposite line and the other went left, the knots leading away but sliding together when their tails were pulled, like two snakes swallowing each other. It works as well for attaching a towline as it does for making a threadborn necklace magically adjustable, and I loved its indifference to scale. It also felt like a secret way into the rites of deckhand passage as a girl—a way in which knotcraft felt equally masculine and feminine and in turn made me feel deeply useful, which was rare.

Next came the bowline, the "king of knots," with its remarkable ability to hold fast under any amount of strain and still never seize, always to remain breakable after an incredible load. My father made some attempt at teaching me about rabbits and trees and holes, but I could never remember the story, and still can't. It was not a rabbit; it was an end of a line, and it was clear to me what made it work or fail, so I learned to tie it by shape rather than by story. Knowing how to spell and pronounce it felt every bit as important as tying it, another occult word handed down from old sailors, like *gunwhale*, and *forecastle*, and *boatswain* (pronounced "gunnel," "folk's hole" or "folksel," and "bozun.").

The one I still have to think about to this day is the lowly clove hitch, a miraculously simple loop that is nonetheless able to hold a several-ton boat in place against a cleat on a dock. I often have to turn it one way and then the next to remember which way will make a clove and which will give me a cow hitch, like a pretzel. The less I think about it, the more likely I am to get it right. Physics says clove hitches work thanks to the ratio of the rope to the diameter of the thing around which it is wrapped—a thread clove-hitched to a finger will slip, but the thick lines of boats hold fast to their relatively narrow ties, a trick of friction that most boat people know intuitively.

While sailing and navigation prior to the digital age required a much more exhaustive and ornate vocabulary of knots than on contemporary diesel vessels, fishermen still use many of the traditional loops that have been holding fast for thousands of years. In this way, knots are like rituals of the hands that have been passed down for countless generations, binding and catching with gesture and shape. We learn by watching, by touching the lines, by somebody showing us how.

Like any guild where knowledge is power, there is often a hierarchy of important work on a boat, the skilled labor of mechanics or gear work versus grunt tasks like cleaning the bilge. Knowledge is sought after, and a master and apprentice relationship often develops based on how many knots a person knows to tie well and how useful those knots are perceived to be.

The most basic are the simple knots of strength—even as a child, I was taught how to hang a corkline and counted on to make my careful way the length of the webloft, wrapping and cinching with the thick white twine as I went, the ping of the needles a punctuation to our work. Similarly, late autumn nights were often spent in front of the TV with a nailed board between our knees, tying ganions, or longline knots, for the halibut season. They didn't have to be pretty; they just had to be strong.

More complex are the intricacies of web, the quick and precise constellations of knots and lengths measured with uncanny exactness by the fingers. True masters of this are part spider, part machine. We once had a deckhand named Jesse who was a sorcerer of the craft, his hands flying over tears in the net in a blur, creating perfectly taut web and repairing holes before the rest of us could even find a three-bar. But Jesse lamented the amount of rice we ate on the boat and missed his wife and so returned to his native Ireland after a season or two to become a seine builder, taking his net wizardry with him.

I learned to sew by holding the web for my father, who, besides Jesse, was the fastest and the most precise. He was exacting in how he wanted it held as well—always a little higher than was comfortable for me, so my arms and shoulders ached, and he grew impatient when I fell behind his progress or failed to hold it at just the right tension. So I watched carefully, gathering and dropping the web as we went along the length of a tear, holding it just so and bracing against his yanks that tugged each knot true, ensuring it would never slip and would hold its diamond along with thousands of others as they formed their invisible wall in the water. In this way, I learned to sew—upside down and backward—but it helped me learn to think in three dimensions and to turn shapes in my mind.

When I was finally trusted to take the needle and yank the knots tight on my own, I was nearly as fast and precise as he was. This created no small edge of conflict on deck, when I, the teenage girl, was given the dubious honor of doing the net-mending work over the fumbling hands of grown men. A few calculated errors could have relieved me of this job, if I'd thought about it, sent me inside to the galley to do the cooking instead, but my pride kept my knife and needle fast and sure. I didn't want to be the skipper's daughter. I wanted to be a good deckhand. I wanted to be an adept.

The most intricate of knots are also, perhaps, the least obviously useful. These are the knots that are more decorative than functional, knots that I imagine are the result of long years at sea and few creative outlets at hand. I knew a friendly, aimless man who wandered the docks in Kodiak. He lacked the sharpness of mind to make it any longer as a deckhand, but he busied himself tying macramé cigarette lighter holders out of mending twine for any women who would talk to him in the bar. He had come across a water-stained, spine-popped copy of the sailor bible known as the *Ashley Book of Knots* and was determined to learn every single entry it contained, proudly showing me his versions of such elaborate wonders as the pineapple knot and the coveted monkey fist. We had a monkey fist on our boat, for throwing the end of the towline from skiff to deck when we closed up every set. It had never occurred to me that someone, not a machine, had had to actually tie it, once upon a time. These knots baffled and impressed me, though they occurred to me less as

magic and more as parlor tricks to wow and to amuse. Their elaborate wraps did make knife handles more dependable, however, and I
longed for a Turks head to wear around my wrist. I knew the thick,
robust weave of dark twine would be the envy of other girls who
grew bored with the fussy threads of friendship bracelets.

Now that I am no longer fishing, I find I miss the vocabulary
of knots, miss the subtle ways I could signal my competence by
how quickly I could tie off onto a cleat or mend a tear in the bag. I
miss having the opportunity to let the old rituals pass through me,
through my hands, to work their powers in the material world.

At the same time, I seek out opportunities to use them, and in
doing so, feel like I'm passing briefly between worlds. My landlubber
Portland friends don't see the girl on deck who didn't weigh enough
to hold the purse line taut. They see a boat person, tying a rope with
a secret shape they'd never have thought of. They see things secured
safely to the roof of their car with maybe a little too much flair. My
child sees that the necklace they made now has an adjustable back,
and they're delighted they can wear it tight but still take it easily
off. And I see everything that knots have taught me: that there are
always ways to learn, and that the work of my hands has meaning;
that sometimes patience and gentleness is the only way out of a mess;
that some things will break under tension, and stress makes things
harder to be undone. And that strength and utility come in many
unexpected shapes.

9

Shell

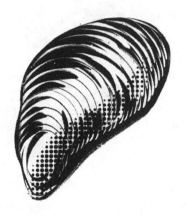

I.

WHEN THE LAND AND THE OCEAN MEET, they speak with many voices and arrive in many moods. Standing on the shore, I imagine the babble and pidgins of trade routes intersecting, the polyglot marketplace hubbub of crossroads, water travelers coming to trade with the people of stone and the couriers of wind. No two beaches sound exactly the same. Some waves gnaw at the sand, crunching it ever finer and swallowing it back with the tide; others hurl their shoulders against the pits and crags of rocks, gathering and exploding in rhythmic smash. Some creep up the stony edge with myriad wet fingers, then hiss in retreat, tumbling small stones as they slide. Underfoot, some beaches tick and chime as their stones roll and strike; others clatter like handfuls of coins. Still others whisper as their sand is tossed in the wind or hush and squelch as they cave and flood with every footstep.

I keep my gaze downward as I walk on a beach. Sometimes it's to pick my way across uneven terrain or to steer clear of wet algae. Mostly it's about treasure-seeking. Walking on beaches is never about a destination—I'm never trying to get from one specific point to another, or with any great speed. It's about being there, on the edge of the infinite, staring out into the closest thing to a straight line that nature has to offer, the water horizon. And it's about seeing what is there, beneath my feet.

Beachcombing is like finding magic-eye patterns; from the noise of complex visual static, a new image emerges suddenly, visible and plain where nothing was moments before. My eyes travel across the surface of the beach underfoot, gliding past millions upon millions of tiny stones, crystals, grains of sand, shells, bits of seaweed and crabs with every step. How does the eye find what it's looking for? Is it novelty that draws attention to itself, an unusual color or shape? Or maybe it is that some shells are simply more perfect than others—their very shellness describing an ideal form—and so it is in their similarity to all other shells, to the *idea* of a shell, or a stone, or a feather, whatever type of prize it is I have found, that it becomes special, a thing to be treasured.

The act of beachcombing is a form of meditation all its own. It requires patience and a slow pace. It demands a particular kind of looking and seeing, a submission to the powers of serendipity and attention. I let my eyes relax and find things through intuition and some other, less accessible process of beholding. Like water divining, I follow the ground and trust the idea that there are shapes and colors that simply want to be found. I wait to hear the shell's voice or the pebble's. Some seem to want to stay right where they are. Others long to travel—to be flung back into the water or to be pocketed for some adventure. Sometimes I pick one up only to find that it wants to be set back down before I leave the beach, as if it only wanted to keep me company for a while, or it needed a lift a few hundred yards down. Either way, knowing what feels right to take and to leave involves a great deal of listening.

One of the reasons beachcombing feels so reflective is because it involves moving with intention through a liminal zone. The beach is not a hard boundary. The ocean is not a wall. The intertidal line between shore and sea shifts constantly and sometimes violently; what was once underwater can later be many yards away from the edge of the waves—and what was sure, dry land can quickly be submerged, rendered deadly or unreachable. That shifting of zones makes it wild and if not exactly unpredictable, then unknowable in the way of a person whose moods swing with precipitous angles. Is this place for me, or not for me? What manner of place is it, after all?

In the swell and recession of the water's edge, we are granted small pockets of mystery—glimpses into the spaces we can never inhabit. Tide pools allow us to peer and poke, to wonder at the complex, miniature lives that take place directly under the surface, often hidden from our view. Entire worlds are caught in cups and bowls within the rocks, where beings swirl and chase and skitter and hide. Underwater grasses hang like tired hair from their stone anchors at low tide. Barnacles clench tight against the dry air, waiting for the waves to return and bring with them their tiny food.

In this liminal zone, creatures and objects from one world can be stranded in the other. Trash from the dry world gets tossed into the ocean and then spit back out onto the beaches. Land things spend time at sea and are returned, rendered strange and round and new: driftwood bleaches pale and grows soft on the edges; bottles shatter and tumble and are returned as sea glass, jewels with curved edges that only shine when wet; bones crack and grow woodlike; feathers become stiff and flightless, sticky sharp arrows and tiny sandcastle flags. Water things get left behind when the tide recedes: crab carapaces like brittle pink stones; kelp forming long, rubbery snakes in the sand; leaping fleas; jellyfish hardened to blobs of jam; bubbles and foam, the sea aggravated to froth on the beach. It is these marooned objects that we gather and assemble into collections and mobiles, that we dangle from strings or fill our pockets, attempting to carry some of the feeling of the liminal zone back home with us.

II.

My parents met in a bar in Kodiak called the Beachcombers. Though it later moved into a building nearby, at the time, it was a repurposed passenger ship, the F/V *Beachcomber*, and served as a hotel, restaurant, and dance club—the crown jewel of Kodiak nightlife in the 1960s. My mom was staying in one of the rooms, while my dad was living on the roof in a sleeping bag, looking for work on the cannery beach gang. It was a cheap date: women were scarce in Kodiak in those days, and free drinks filled the bar in front of her. They stopped counting at forty-five. A man at a nearby table had ordered a pork chop dinner and then promptly passed out in his seat. Not wanting to see a meal go to waste, my dad carefully lifted the man's face from the plate and offered the pork chops to my mom. They shared. Times were tight, and thrift was an attractive quality.

The term *beachcomber* entered common vocabulary through Herman Melville's book *Omoo*, referring to individuals and communities of usually English sailors who abandoned ship in the South Pacific and adopted the lives of beach bums. The name became synonymous with hobo or criminal—probably because deserters were treated harshly when they were caught—but also acquired the sense of scavenger, connoting a person who gleaned from beaches things of utility or for trade, and who lived off coastal fishing and barter. Some acted as bounty hunters, turning in fellow deserters for their rewards. Many of these original beachcombers, who numbered in the thousands in the South Pacific during the mid-nineteenth century, were incorporated into island life, and some even transitioned into careers as merchants once their trade relationships grew established.

Beachcombing still retains a bit of the scavenger mindset at times—we look not only for shells and stones, things of beauty, but also bits and pieces of function, reclaimed utility. For a time, the glass balls used as floats by the Japanese and Koreans would wash up on beaches, some buried in sand like gleaming blue or brown eggs, others still bound in their seine-bearing mesh. Fish roe boxes often wash up intact, their characters and stamps like messages from far away. Jugs, hooks, bits of line, mysteriously shaped pieces of metal, healthy lengths of cord, old floats and buoys—so much returns to the shore that can be used again. What we choose to scavenge says so much about us, about what we value and find precious and worth rescuing.

My mother found small things. She had a gift for discovering beauty where it was least expected—in a knot, a twist of wood, a curve of seaweed. She loved things with print, things that carried the ghosts of a story inside them, things that had once clearly been useful and personal. She taught me to find wonder by paying attention to the tiny, the complex, and the lovely—to allow things to be beautiful simply for their own sake. She would arrange small collections of objects in bowls or on windowsills. These collections functioned like collages or still lifes; they seemed to be far greater than the sum of their parts, as if careful contemplation of the arranged objects would reveal some greater truth about them or form a rhyme, a melody, or a joke. These temporary altars would appear and disappear around the boat, and in our home—quiet, tiny installations that elevated the sense of value and beauty in all the things around us. Basic objects took on the power to become art.

My father found big things. He taught me that scavenging can be epic. He dragged an enormous piece of driftwood shaped like a ten-foot phallus and balls from a beach in Uganik Bay and then arranged to drive it all the way down south to our winter home in eastern Oregon, where he erected it in the driveway. He later nailed a birdhouse to the side of the shaft. First-time guests were never sure if they were supposed to see it as the huge penis that it so clearly was and the looks of discomfort or amusement were quick litmus tests of personality.

Another summer, we watched a beached whale slowly decompose over the course of the season. When it had finally reduced to a skeleton, he took a skiff to the beach and chained up the jawbone, dragging it back to the boat and winching it aboard. He carried the bone all the way south to Seattle, then mounted it across a truck and drove it, too, to eastern Oregon. It sat in the front yard—all twelve feet of it—for years, until one day, when a man from the FBI arrived with a manila folder containing Polaroids of the entire process and a warrant to reclaim the bone.

Not all scavenging is about aesthetics or display, however. In some places, beachcombing is more about repurposing and recycling the colossal amounts of trash that wash up on the shore, the detritus of consumer culture left for others to deal with. Every bit of garbage that goes overboard or is tossed where it can float or drift to the ocean is treated as if the ocean were infinite. It is as if humans imagine the ocean is capable of absorbing all the abuse we have to offer, its depths and breadth untouchable by human waste and mismanagement.

When I was a kid, it was common for us to throw bags of garbage overboard with exactly this mindset. We would dutifully punch holes in the tops and bottoms of cans to ensure they would sink; the truly progressive among us might even snip the plastic loops that held six-packs together to prevent strangling seagulls or small seals, but once these small gestures at mindfulness had been made, the whole lot would end up in a plastic bag and go overboard. I learned early on how to make an oil slick disappear: drizzle dish soap over the top of it to weigh it down. If the oil sinks, no one will ever know it was there.

The habit of throwing trash overboard cost us in personal ways. My parents were poor when they got engaged; my dad famously proposed with a rubber Green Hornet ring he'd gotten out of a plastic ball from a vending machine. It took years for them to earn the money for a fancier wedding ring, but once they did, he commissioned a custom gold band for my mother, wrought with twisting golden vines and set with real rubies. It was a beautiful, unusual ring. One sunny afternoon, we were fishing at Bird Bluffs—a place where a vast rock wall rises sheer and straight from the water, streaked in white and home to thousands of noisy terns, puffins, and murres. My mother was in the cabin, cleaning something, and slid open the galley window to toss a paper towel overboard. With the force of this gesture, the ring slipped from her wet finger and flew over the side. The paper towel floated like an origami gull, wadded and indifferent, while her beautiful ring plopped and sank below the surface, never to be reclaimed. We still make heartbroken jokes about the treasure buried at Bird Bluffs.

Though these waste practices have not been commonplace in Alaska for decades, the ocean continues to be used as a waste dump globally, both for trash and for emissions of every pollutant imaginable: nuclear, chemical, carbon. The Pacific Ocean now hosts two enormous floating rafts of plastic garbage—refuse, fishing nets, and the dumped contents of shipping containers, primarily—known as the Great Pacific Garbage Patch, or the Pacific Trash Vortex. In 2019 the total area of the trash vortex and its periphery spanned 1.6 million square kilometers, with the densest regions measuring twice the size of Texas and nine feet deep. This number is expected to double over the next ten years. These plastics do not biodegrade but rather break down into ever smaller microplastics, which in turn can be ingested by marine life. In fact, these plastics—most of which are toxic—are already found in around 10 percent of the fish living in the region. In the gyre itself, the swirl of currents that bring the trash vortices together, there is six times more plastic than plankton, the fundamental component of the marine food chain. Similar garbage patches exist in the Atlantic and the Mediterranean as well.

Marine law has very specific delineations regarding who can claim what from a shipwreck. *Flotsam* refers to those things that accidentally fall overboard and float away; *jetsam* (from "jettison,") refers to things that were thrown. *Lagan* are those things that are intentionally jettisoned, as well, but which sink below the surface, possibly marked by a buoy or a line. *Derelict* is the name for objects that sink or are trapped within a vessel, with no hope of ever being recovered. Flotsam must be returned to the original owner, while jetsam is the property of whoever finds it. Who, then, is responsible for the waste that is now so vast that it is forming its own continents in the oceans? Who will lay claim to the flotsam and jetsam of the great sinking ship of our relationship to the natural world, to the oceans and all that live there?

III.

Mollusks, like clams, oysters, and mussels, have hard shells that are unlike those of land-based shelled creatures, like tortoises. They are not formed by cells, and they do not have circulatory systems inside them. Instead, they are like concrete bunkers formed by layering calcium carbonate over thin architectural structures of proteins. The mollusk slowly adds layers as it grows, giving its shell the ridges or color patterns that you can see once the shell has been emptied. In this way, shells are similar to the rings of trees—the growth evident in the overlapping concentric patterns formed over time. Different shapes of shells serve different protective purposes. Simple cold-water clam shells are tough but heavy. The more elaborate shell shapes in tropical zones, with their swoops and spikes and whorls, are thought to be defense against the more intense predation that occurs in tropical waters. Heavy shells are hard to move around; the more ornate, corrugated shapes are difficult to break and lighter to carry.

In order for marine animals to build their shells (like oysters and clams) or exoskeletons (like corals or lobsters), they must engage in some finely tuned chemistry. They make their own tough primary building material by extracting carbonate from the surrounding seawater and combining it with calcium. However, they have a challenge: hydrogen ions also bond with carbonate ions, so marine shell-builders have to get rid of hydrogen when they are working on their shell or exoskeleton so that the carbonate is available to them for their own project. Researchers think they do this by creating little "proton pumps" that drive out hydrogen and create pockets of ionized calcium and carbonate so the two can bond and form new shell material.

Besides dumping colossal amounts of trash, humans are flooding the oceans with another form of pollution: carbon dioxide, from the emissions that come from burning fossil fuels. The oceans act as a vast carbon sink, drawing in CO_2 from the atmosphere. At first, this discovery seemed like a boon to climate scientists, who recognized that the absorption of CO_2 by seawater meant less in the air, which could slow the warming of the Earth's overall temperature. However, it was quickly realized that this absorption has effects of its own. As the carbon dioxide dissolves in water, carbonic acid is formed.

The more carbon dioxide that is absorbed, the more the ocean's pH drops, becoming closer to acidic—thus, the process is known as "ocean acidification." Since the start of the Industrial Revolution, the ocean has become 30 percent more acidic, the fastest ocean chemistry change in fifty million years.

The effects of this rapid shift are still not well understood. It is likely that some marine life will thrive under warmer, more acidic conditions. Others—like corals and most other shell-producing animals—will not. Carbonic acid has an eroding effect on calcium carbonate shells. Simply put, the shells slowly dissolve in the more acidic waters, much like the school science experiment of dissolving a chicken bone in a glass of coke. Furthermore, when carbonic acid is formed, hydrogen ions are released and bond with the existing carbonate in the seawater, making it less available for shell production. This also increases the amount of energy organisms must expend on building their shells, using proton pumps or other mechanisms, making it more difficult for them to rebuild or restore their shells after damage.

Not all marine shell-builders will be at a loss. Some crustaceans—lobsters, prawns, and blue crabs, for instance—demonstrate an ability to build stronger shells with the increase of carbon in the water. This suggests that the makeup of the oceans is likely to shift radically in the coming years. Calcifying algae, mussels, limpets, and crustaceans may thrive. Meanwhile conches, corals, urchins, snails, clams, oysters, and scallops may disappear entirely, along with all the other parts of the ecosystem that depend upon them for food or shelter, from tiny zooplankton to sea otters.

What might a beach look like in a hundred years, when there are no more shells? What will the scavengers, the beachcombers find then? Stones and carapaces, driftwood, endless bits of plastic. When the odd shell that hasn't dissolved or been tumbled to sand turns up, will it want to be found? Perhaps it will have a tiny voice asking to be collected, to be rescued from the acid waters from which it came.

Or maybe it will simply lie unnoticed beneath layers of trash, one more small shape among millions, its shellness no longer pointing to anything in the real world.

I imagine a child a century from now, stooping to pluck a perfect clam shell from the sand, puzzling over its flawless shape and ridges. Would they think they had found a fossilized wing? A fairy's dish? Perhaps they would know what it was and clutch it breathlessly, thrilled as if they had found a tiny dinosaur bone, an impossible thing from the past. I wonder if we will remember seashells even after they are gone, if we will mourn them and wish we had done things differently. As with what we scavenge, what we choose to protect says so much about us, about what we value and find precious and worth rescuing.

10

Light

IN THE FIRST OF THE FIVE SKY WORLDS live the moon and stars, say the Alutiiq, who have known every corner of Kodiak for thousands upon thousands of years. The moon is a man who walks the sky at night wearing a glowing mask, his face beaming down onto the earth below. He fell in love with a woman from the land and married her, brought her to the sky world, where they lived together happily, mostly. But night after night, the man waited until her breathing settled into dreams, then he crept out of their bed and left her. The woman grew increasingly jealous and angry when he would not tell her where he went, so she resolved to follow him, to catch him in the acts she imagined as she lay in bed alone, only pretending to sleep.

He stole through the door of their dwelling one night, and she waited a few moments before trailing after him. He entered a small hut and left again. When she was sure he was gone, she went in to see what was more important than the warm bed they shared.

What she saw made her breath catch. Though the hut was dim and full of shadows, she was surrounded by gleaming, polished masks, faces of every phase of the moon, each slightly larger or smaller than the last. She ran her fingers across their bright surfaces, awed and enchanted, and selected one, nearly round; she lifted it off its hook on the wall and placed it gently upon her face. It gripped at her, and she clawed at it, but it stuck fast. She was unable to remove it and retreated to her home and bed, terrified, her face a gleaming disc. When her husband returned, she confessed to what she had done, to spying on the tools of the sky god. From that point forward, she had to help her husband with his work, walking across the skies when it was time for her mask to beam down upon the lands and the ice and the waters.

In a land of reflection, what is the meaning of light?

I see her face, pale and full and nearly round, radiant but full of gray shadows. I stand far below, stranded in the liminal space between water and sky, the deck a weak facsimile of earth beneath my feet. The ocean extends from our hull in a great plain, like a desert's wild dream of itself.

The moon's path paints a bright stripe, our wake mimicking its shape in froth and color, a rare event taking place in the water around us. A line of vivid green snakes out behind us, impossibly lit as if struck by a wand, the gleam of it a cloud of microscopic droplets, tiny bioluminescent organisms flashing and flaring like a storm of sparks, their collective flicker merged into a hazy glow.

Luciferin, scientists call this. Light-bringer. Illuminating only when disturbed, *Stay away*, these lights say, beautiful in their function, warning off potential predators of the dinoflagellates who produce them. Or maybe *Over here!* to the predators of their predators, a visible signal that the enemy of their enemy is a friend.

In the dark of early morning, well after the midsummer brightness has faded to a brief dip into black, the other deckhand and I stand on the hatch covers, staring into the gleaming wake as the net gallops off the stern. Once it has gone out, I flip the switch that activates the deck pump, sending gallons of sea water churning through the hose. Sparks scatter across the deck like bright marbles, green cat eyes skittering and spilling through the scuppers. I point the hose at the shoulder of my raingear and watch tiny motes of light dance the length of my arm, my gloved fingertips dripping beads of green flame. I chase the seaweed and scales and muck from the grit of the deck with the water, sluicing it clean while laughing and splashing at the motes, like washing with infinitesimal pixies.

Once the net has gone out, the other deckhand detaches a long aluminum plunger pole with a cup on the end from the side of the boat and we take turns plunging, slamming the cup into the water at the stern. We plunge to mimic the dive of a seal, frightening fish from the gap between the net and the boat, the sound a wet *thock*, a spulge of bubbles, another flare of light.

Predator! the dinoflagellates flash.

But we are the predators; the tiny water pixies are not our prey.

There is a light that is neither day nor night, a long stretch of purple that fades into morning the color of driftwood. This purple space carries us from one day to the next without rest, a slow alarm like the arrival of waves. It is ceaseless, cyclic, blooming and fading, the depths of the dark only a brief opportunity to see those more distant lights of stars, of the magnetic fields dancing at the poles. These glimmers remind me we are always in darkness, darkness is the state around us, and it is only the bounce of energy that renders things sensible.

Without our eyes, what is the meaning of light?

Rare, clear sun means blindness. Light strikes the water, broken or twisting. On a bright day, wave patterns like a thousand tiny mountain ranges each split into a thousand peaks, a fractal explosion of wavelets with countless edges and facets for the light to shatter itself against. Shards ricochet into our eyes, and we squint against it like a shower of shrapnel. On cloudy days, the light slants through, and the surface is mercury, smooth and looping, shadows interlocking and chasing one another like knotted dragons, like endless returns.

Though the light is often pale, filtered through haze and the thick layers of mist that guard us from the sun and from warmth, its relentless presence pounds into our skin nonetheless, like waves against stone, slowly wearing away the surface and leaving it weathered and rough, leathery against spray and squint. As if we raised masks of salt and found they could never be removed. Glare bounces from sky to water and back again, the exposure above and below. As opening to sunlight renders a negative dark, so does the light burn into our faces and leave us tanned despite the cold on our skin. Spying on the tools of the sun.

When darkness arrives, what is the meaning of light?

In the days before we had a wheelhouse, night traveling was done from the cabin, wheelwatch held in the captain's chair, a short hop from the galley table, with its rubber-mesh top that gathered crumbs and goo and kept our plates and cribbage board from sliding with the swell. I could span it with an arm, though I rarely reached over that direction for fear of bumping the panel of Very Important Switches that led to the fo'c'sle where orange lights gleamed like faceted bee's eyes and small red lights stayed dark unless something bad happened.

Running at night meant the crew could sleep, or read, or rest. A red bulb overhead smoked the galley in a ruby glow like a darkroom, allowing wheelwatch vision to stay sharp for marker buoys and the running lights of other vessels. It rendered the space weird, sometimes nightmarish in times of tension or rough seas, playful and dreamlike when there was laughter or music or curling tendrils of smoke setting everyone at ease. Green light from the radar whirled against pale faces nestled into the rubber cuff; the traveling wand of the ping drew pallid radii against the glassy surfaces of their eyes. Light shows us the way across dark waters when the sky god is at rest.

The crew nestles into the clammy confines of their bunks, sometimes lit by flashlight for reading, or the glow of a watch, or the cheery shine of a clamp light, some with small curtains tugged tight for privacy and to keep the light in. The bunks are tiny damp kingdoms, secret domains for stashed candy bars, girlie mags, a shortwave radio beaming staticky voices in Russian or the lilting, otherworldly tones of the BBC.

After a long time out fishing, the lights of town or cannery appear like a promise from the dark—the deeper shadows of capes and rocks and trees giving way to dots of light in the distance, glimmers of movement and whispers of civilization: showers, laundry, fresh vegetables, a chance to stretch one's legs.

Standing on deck, I watch planes glide silently overhead, their distant blinks as removed as alien craft, yet reminders of other places, other friends and faces and concerns. Mail comes by plane, hand-writing and care packages of cocoa and newspapers. People leave, go back home to other jobs, to warmth, to frequent showers or less demanding work. Satellites glint past, busy sending the noise of information from one side of the world to the other, cold and remote. These lights trace dotted lines, connecting us back to our other worlds, reminding us of other lives, other people we know or get to be once we, too, leave this place.

When the line between night and day is thin, what is the meaning of light?

The endless midsummer daylight makes more work possible, no circadian clocks allowed to time us in and out of our labors, just light and more light coaxing us to the fishing grounds, igniting the spurt of energy that starts our day, the extra chemical boost that leads us to grind, set after set. The splash of water and breeze the constant slap needed to stay alert and present in the work, to shrug off the hypnotic lull of the mechanical rhythms, the lullaby of repetition numbing the body and leaving the mind to wander.

In the scant late summer hours between pitch and daylight, when shadows are ink against black, fish continue to move. The deck lights blare surfaces in high contrast and carve deep shadows behind objects, the thick sheen on wet raingear, the glint on trapped scales, the shine and glare from places where the lights bounce on flat water, the harsh and vivid relief of faces behind hoods, grimacing up at the net against salt water and the flood of light. We create daylight to continue the work, to flood our own systems with the cortisol needed to stay in motion, to beat back the hum of sleep that drags at our limbs and eyes.

At last we make our way back to the sheltered harbor of a bay where the tender awaits. I lie on the net in raingear, not quite in repose but definitely in rest, the in-between, desperate, joyful rest of knowing that we won't be making another set, yet choosing to stay wet rather than slide back into the cold muck of boots when we offload.

We glide alongside to deliver, slipping up with quiet stealth compared to the clamor and splash of the tender operation—the urgent buzz of hydraulics in motion, the deafening whirr of engines and pumps, the shout of orders, the clang of brailers, and the whoosh of dead fish, the occasional slap of life leaving metallic bodies, like liquid silver pouring from reeking pink foam. The spatter is everywhere, sequin scales clinging to odd surfaces, lending an air of glamour to strange and filthy objects—a deck brush, a winch, a sodden wooden floorboard. The lights fall onto the deck like trumpet blasts, an entire brass section honking white light over every surface, the glare of it sending all work and grit and sludge and speckle into high contrast, cutting tiny dark shadows behind the smallest edge, overlapping with other lights, other angles, all there to fuel the work—as the fishermen are ending their day, the tender workers are beginning, scampering here and there and tying off lines, tossing buoys to cushion the pulling alongside, writing out tickets in exchange for poundage, sharing produce, fuel, or water—a small floating marketplace, dedicated to the cannery, a waterbound company store. When we cast off, their lights recede, and with them, the noise and the pace.

It's a delicious thing, the moment when we anchor up, when the engine noise stops and the silence rolls from my shoulders like caramel. I strip off the clammy wraps of plastic, the gurry-soaked cuffs and the wet; I hang salt-soaked sleeves over a makeshift clothesline near the galley stove, change into precious dry socks, put on a stiff sweatshirt with stinking sleeves, and then eat and finally, finally rest.

I brush my teeth on deck, taking what space for myself I can find. I feel rather than hear a ringing that prickles my skin like static. My eyes are pulled upward. Eerie green bands waver and dance across the sky, impossibly large and grand and terrifying. The ribbons of light are nearly audible in their wave, a ringing, vast closeness brought down to earth. The Alutiiq say these lights are the spirits of those who died in battle. Warriors join the star and moon spirits in the first of the five sky worlds, and the green aurora are these warriors' spirits coming out to play. They illuminate the night for their families below, who believe they can whistle them down.

I feel a shrinking, my small animal soul fearing the end of days in the face of such wild power. It is as if the bands reach into my chest and draw the thinking parts of me out, heave them upward, and scatter them across the surface of the water. I stare and try to breathe.

The light means folk.

The light means seeking.

The light means *I am here*.

11

Skiff

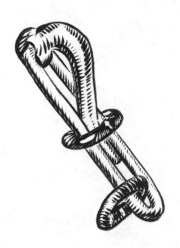

NOT ALL CREW ARE CREATED EQUAL. In the hierarchy of the boat, the skipper is at the top—a pinnacle so steep and high that he is seldom even visible from deck, secure in the wheelhouse or on the flying bridge like a god tucked away in the clouds—unless the net is coming in, then he is on deck, directing the operation like a conductor. The only crew who approaches that level of importance is the skiffman. The rest of the us are just deck monkeys, as we were often called, hands for hauling in the net and doing all the pulling and coiling and stacking that needs to be done in a fishing operation but with none of the decision-making or strategy that goes into when and where the net gets set. Deckhands are the muscle; the skiffman is the brains. For this job, the skiffman typically earns up to twice the percentage of a deckhand, especially if the deckhand is a greenhorn.

The skiffman drives his own boat—the skiff—and stays in it nearly all the time. He is allowed out under three circumstances: on the rare occasion when there is a line of boats waiting to put their nets in the same place for a set, when emergency gear work needs to be done by as many hands as possible, and at the end of the day during delivery. The rest of the time, he stays in the skiff. The skiffman eats in the skiff, pisses over the side of the skiff, and sometimes even hangs his ass off the edge if need be—but he stays there, just in case the net has to go out. And once the net's out, there he is at the far end, a quarter mile away, helping to hold the hanging wall of seine in the water like a hook.

The skiffman and the skipper stay in close communication via radio and hand signals, communicating about where the fish are, the direction they're traveling, the speed and movement of the tide, and other considerations (what they want for dinner, what their balls feel like, what they'll do when they get back to town). Once the skipper signals the end of the tow, either by making a giant O overhead with his arms, or muttering, "close 'er up" into the radio, the skiffman begins hauling the far end of the net back to the boat. When it reaches the boat, the net has made an enormous circle around the fish, and there is a frenzied handoff of lines on deck, allowing the crew to begin pulling the net in over the hydraulic block. Another line is attached to the stern or the side of the boat, with which the skiffman then tows the big boat around the net, making it easier to haul in, and keeping the boat from drifting over the top of it and releasing the fish or snagging web in the wheel.

This level of attention and decision-making often leads to skiff-men becoming skippers themselves. At the very least, the best skip-pers were generally skiffmen at one time. My dad was crew and then drove skiff. He says he learned a lot out there—about angles and fish and also about how to handle other skippers.

Because of the importance of the skiff in the operation, skiffmen are often the recipients of more than their fair share of abuse on behalf of the skipper, but they are also farther away than the deck-hands, who tend to absorb the impact of it more directly. Skippers tend to come in two styles: gentlemen and screamers, and my dad was well known as being one of the finest of the latter. In one infamous set during a hectic opener at Red River, he had frothed himself into such a histrionic rage screaming at the skiffman that he was literally jumping up and down on his hat, his face red and eyes bulging, as an eloquent stream of curse belted forth at top volume, striking every-where across the deck like dirty lightning. He jumped and shrieked and gestured so wildly that he fell down into the hatch, breaking a rib. The purse line began piling over his head before a deckhand was able to vault over the net and turn off the hydraulics. Meanwhile, the skiffman just drowned it all out with a touch more throttle.

In the old days, there was no throttle. The Norwegians who established much of the early commercial industry in Alaska (not including the long-standing subsistence fishing practiced by the various Native nations for thousands of years) had no engines in their skiffs and no hydraulics on deck. They used rowboats and pulleys and sheer muscle and determination. It's hard to imagine that same work being accomplished without mechanical assistance—the amount of strength required to do that work unaided or the arms that work would produce.

For many years, outboards were what moved the skiff, and while they were an enormous step up from rowing, they had their limitations as well. Once jet skiffs were introduced, seiners were able to get closer to the beach, work in heavier seas, and pull in nets faster. Everything in the industry tended toward more work, more productivity. At the same time, the work of the skiffman grew easier. All he has to do is sit or stand at the controls and watch for fish. Occasionally, he might plunge. But the job has become a soft one, and skiffmen often gain weight over the season, eating like the rest of the crew but without the constant burn of stacking net and deck work. Most only get exercise while pitching fish. Some skiffmen are very sensitive about this, the two-edged sword of their elevated status: they make more money but leave the season without the powerful physique of a deckhand.

We had the same skiffman for most of my childhood—Don, a man my father had grown up with in southern Indiana. He was like an uncle to me, heavyset, unshaven, a mind full of ceaseless trivia and mental puzzles, a dirty sense of humor, and a bandana on his head. Don struggled with his body image and with the rough treatment he received from my father as skipper—a dynamic that must have strained their old friendship—but he loved fishing, and he had his own ways of handling the screaming. "It just goes in one ear and out the other," he said to me and my mother once after a particularly difficult day. "Just let it go through you. Don't let it stick."

We had other skiffmen over the years after Don retired to stay down south and teach. I felt like the family was breaking apart, but I liked the influence of new people—most of the time.

Some were cocky, distant, superior. When they came on deck, they'd immediately go up topside and lounge on the flying bridge, installing themselves as accessory to the skipper, at leisure and at his command, like a prized hound. Others were kind and brilliant and quiet, had soft accents and brought stories from the other side of the world. I learned about how big the world was by listening to them, by gathering these stories, like living at a crossroads or trading post.

Still others were disgusting but good at their jobs. One man nicknamed himself after an animal. He ate like a pig and prided himself on sounding gross at all times. My dad loved him because he could do his own work on the skiff, but he was always unbearable to me, suggestive and leering, belching, nasty. He'd be working on the engine and say, "Hey Lara, come back here and give me a hand. I've got a big greasy bolt here I need you to wrap your fingers around."

Fishing work is full of negative reinforcement. The best in the skiff are only clearly the best because there is the least amount of screaming; it can be hard to tell if someone is particularly skilled because there is rarely any praise. Things can only go wrong, never right. On deck, we kept our fingers crossed that each new person in the skiff would be a good one, not just to make more money, but to keep things less volatile for everyone.

As I got older, everyone always asked when I was going to run skiff. They'd stumble over the gendered language—"Why aren't you skiffman, er—woman? Skiffperson?" It was funny to me that they could hear it in the job title associated with the work, but that it was often invisible in "fisherman." I disliked attempts to fix it, though—awkward gestures like "fisher," or "skiff operator" only served to underscore the markedness of my sex. I was content to be a fisherman, but I didn't want to be a skiffman.

"I don't know how," I'd say. And this was true. I didn't know how to run a skiff; I barely knew enough to take wheelwatch on long trips in calm weather. I'd be given a heading and told to aim for it. It took me a long time to get used to the slow, overreactive movements of the boat's steering response. A tiny nudge of the wheel one direction would result in nothing at first, and then a gradual, bobbing turn that felt always somehow inexorable and disastrous, as if the slightest roll would capsize us, or I'd skewer our hull on a pinnacle rock in the middle of Shelikof Strait.

I had been raised with such a sense of danger, such an inflated sense of the importance of machinery—it had kept me safe as a child and makes sense from a parenting perspective—but with it came the certainty that I was utterly incompetent, that it was impossible that I might possess or develop the mechanical savvy to operate a marine vessel with any modicum of confidence or comprehension. I wasn't smart enough, and there were too many mysteries involved. Plus, to run a skiff, I'd have to expose myself to the firehose of criticism and stress that the position entailed. I simply didn't want to be responsible for endangering people's lives and livelihoods, and I wasn't encouraged to feel otherwise.

Besides, I liked being on deck. I liked the strength it required, and I liked knowing I had that strength. I liked the way my arms and shoulders hardened over the course of a summer, liked the fast pace of things, the repetition of things, liked the fact that I could move and jump around, that there were times when all I had to do was complete tasks without thinking too much. On deck, I would space out to the engine vibration and go far down the hole of my thoughts, letting the patterns of the net arrange themselves with my assistance. There were times when all I had to do was hold fast to the purse line and make sure the leads piled neatly.

My mom and I both insisted on an obsessively tidy stack. Other crews would sometimes stop by our boat in the harbor to admire our work; we always made sure we knew when our last set of the day was if we were heading back to town so we could make sure it was especially tight. One deck boss even brought a greenhorn over once, cuffing him upside the head, saying, "See this? THIS is what it's supposed to look like."

The deck was my territory—I knew what had to be done and why, and I felt confident there. Plus, it was more social, so I got to spend time with others. In my late teens, I was deck boss and knew how to respond in nearly every situation, but I was still only a deckhand, the top of the bottom of the pecking order. The skiff was still its own domain, and the skiffman interceded with the skipper like a saint on our behalf. I knew I'd never have that kind of savvy, that kind of sway.

Plus, I was a girl. Despite my mother's experience on deck, I was raised, both implicitly and explicitly, to believe that women were fundamentally mechanically incompetent. I railed against this, craving so badly the knowledge and facility with wrenches and switches and gears that would make me one of the guys, would make me smart. I didn't believe that women were any less competent than men—in fact, I insisted otherwise—but it didn't keep me from doubting my own abilities. The benefit of doubt I was willing to extend to a gender I was unable to grant myself. The women I knew who did run skiff were like superheroes to me, fantasy versions of a self who had crossed over the lines of qualm, who had made it to the true Land of the Competent, who braved the screaming and the burden of fuck-ups and who knew how an engine worked. I longed to be them, but I knew I could never do so on my family boat and opted instead to become the toughest muscle, the quickest thinker, the best with knots and gear. I stuck to my domain, where it was safe.

12

Food

THE IMAGE ON THE BOX shows a young person eagerly eyeing a tall glass of milk being poured. It flows with rich dairy viscosity, fluid lipid goodness in a dense white the color of glue. It looks cold, refreshing—the sort of thing one drinks after eating a particularly chip-laden cookie. However, as I tear open a packet of Milkman powdered milk, the aroma that greets me is curdled, somewhere between caramel and bile. I dump the powder into a plastic jug and then fill it with water from the sink—tepid, funky water that tastes of the tank it has sat in for a week or more. I snap the lid on and shake furiously, forming a thick layer of foam on top. It is neither viscous nor cold. I open it up again and smear the floating lumps with a spoon, creaming them into the plastic. I was once tempted to shake the milk powder directly over my cornflakes and then add water straight to the bowl—an experiment I never repeated. There is little similarity between this sweet-salty froth and the creamy milk I imagined, but there are no alternatives. Once we are on the fishing grounds, we stay there, often for weeks at a time. Fresh milk is a rare treat enjoyed at the cannery, where it comes from a giant metal machine in the mess hall, or circulates like a slushie, next to the box of whirling reconstituted orange juice.

Eventually, they begin irradiating milk and packaging it in foil-lined cartons, cases that we can store up topside in the sun, a technology that produces something more milk-like for my cereal yet also somehow sinister in its longevity and resistance to rot. As fishermen, we are always conscious of the fact that we are acquiring and handling someone's food—the closer something is to its natural state, the better.

Farther down the processing line come chopped, hashed by-products, unrecognizable bits turned into meal and paste. I worry that irradiated milk is the cat food of dairy products. Freshness matters.

"Eat a rainbow," my mother always says. She explains that different vitamins are indicated by different colors, so a full spectrum ensures a balanced diet. She also says, though, that color is beautiful, and it is the job of food to feed the spirit as well as the body. Food can be kept for weeks on a boat—frozen, dried, and canned. The one thing we truly lack is fresh produce, though some things are brought from the cannery by the tender—round, crisp heads of tasteless iceberg, mealy tomatoes, two handfuls of lumpy potatoes. Canned produce quickly loses its vibrancy and becomes pale and soft, ghosts of plants, indicating not only a reduction in value for the body but a collapse of vegetable essence.

~

I run my fingertips along the bunk ceiling above my face. We have been fishing for several weeks straight; our days are often twenty hours long or more, and yet I am suddenly unable to sleep.

"I want a mango," I murmur into the dark.

"There's a mango tree in my backyard at home," comes a voice above me and to the port. It drifts with the soft New Zealand lilt that I love. His name is Ian, and I want him to read me a story, just to hear the angles on his vowels.

The deckhand in the bunk directly overhead turns in his sleeping bag. "I've never had a mango," he confesses. He is from Iowa, where Winnebagos are made.

"What would you eat if we were back in town, Jeff?" I ask. He sighs heavily, thinking.

"Oh, probably some guacamole, with chips. And a beer. A really cold beer."

"I have an avocado tree in my yard too," says Ian. I laugh.

"Bullshit."

"It's true." I can hear him smiling. "And a plum tree, and an Asian pear. There's nothing quite like a properly ripe plum."

I snuggle deeper into my pillow and listen to the skiffman list off the wonders of his garden in his delightful kiwi accent. It is better than a bedtime story. Yesterday, I fell asleep standing up and only awoke when my knees struck the hatch covers. Fruit and sunlight, rest and green leaves—these are the fantasies that compel us.

What we lack in produce we make up for in seafood—salmon whenever we want it, the occasional crab. Jigged halibut or ones that come up in the net. Even octopus, which my six-year-old self remembers with horror as its disembodied arms shoved and writhed and tried desperately to climb out of a boiling pot. Scottie would eat fresh king crab once a summer, like the opposite of Lent. He was wildly allergic and would spend two days after vomiting, but as he said, and anyone who's had fresh king crab with drawn butter knows—it was worth it. Its richness and kaleidoscopic wonder make it the peyote of shellfish. It gave me hallucinatory, geometric dreams, as if I'd eaten the food of the gods on accident and was now subject to their knowledge in ways I couldn't understand. On mellow evenings, we grilled salmon on the hibachi on deck, the smell like coals under rich bronze and cream. If we had time off during closures, these riches gave us a festive sense of bounty and abundance. When we were working, meals had the desperate, necessary quality of a pit stop during a long-distance race.

On the surface, the success of a fishing operation relies upon the skipper, and—to a lesser extent—the skiffman. They decide when and where to set the net, when to close her up, when to keep fishing, and when to stop. The rest of us just move things around and keep the operation in motion. However, the difference between a solid fishing gig and a really excellent one depends not just on the money one earns but on the experience itself. In an occupation with ample breathtaking scenery but few animal comforts, food is not just fuel. It is the heart of social and emotional connection. A good boat cook is a wizard of creativity, portion planning, and time management. They play Iron Chef with dried goods stacked feet deep under galley benches; they anticipate needs and moods and manage to wedge all preparation in during brief breaks between sets, as every cook is also a deckhand. They are the life force of the operation, and they do it all in a tiny kitchen the size of a bathroom stall where everything is in motion. The comfort they provide can make the hard work, the discomfort, and the verbal abuse on deck worthwhile. More than once, I heard from a crewmember, "I just couldn't do this if it weren't for your mom's cooking."

It is not an easy thing to feed a crew of four or five from a galley kitchen. Measuring around nine square feet, space is of the essence, and everything tilts in all planes of rotation. Sturdy plates and bowls are stacked above eye level in cabinets that lock; mugs hang below from hooks shaped in the exact curve the handles follow with the swell. Pots, containers, and vessels all must nest one into another to fit into tiny cupboards and stows. Several weeks' worth of cans and dried goods are squirreled away in cubbies beneath the galley benches. The refrigerator door latches to the wall, and heaven help any hurried deckhand who forgets to secure it, leaving the door to fly open on a big wave. Twine knotted to cup hooks stretches from one wall to the next along the stove pipe, for hanging wet sweatshirts and socks at day's end; the stove hisses as salt water drips down. Like everything else, it reeks of wet wool and drying gurry.

Every fisherman who's been around a while has a story of working with a green cook—food running out halfway through a meal, mountains of fried spam and white bread, or humpies boiled to mush. Having my mom in charge of the galley made us the envy of the fleet. Somehow, with practice and magic and no small amount of cursing, she managed to coax marvels from the little oil stove that coughed and smoked in the corner. Its flat surface served as heat and griddle, gleaming where it had been polished with aluminum foil and grease. Though its temperature settings were basically hot, too hot, and broken, she conjured freshly baked bread, rich lasagna, flakey drop biscuits, and cookies from within its cramped oven, barely wide enough to hold a cookie sheet.

There were no bologna sandwiches on our boat—unless you wanted one. Our little galley produced vats of pasta, piles of waffles, even homemade jam from fruit we'd foraged from the hills. She sent care packages of baked fish, grilled cheese sandwiches with bacon, and toast dripping with butter and honey out to the skiff, their warm foil packets accepted with two-handed gratitude from over the stern. She carried plates heaped with fried chicken, steaming mashed potatoes, and peas up to the wheelhouse with one hand as she climbed a ladder or braced in the stairwell against the swell; in the evenings, she ferried gin and tonics to the skipper. It wasn't just luxury—it was food for the soul.

For crew, food often happens in a rush, eaten standing up or while staring out at the water, looking for jumpers. A deckhand once nearly quit when he discovered we didn't stop for lunch and then worked late into the evening before dinner. When we got close enough to another boat to chat, he leapt aboard and asked when they ate, sure that our schedule was cruel and unusual.

"We eat when the work's done!" growled the other skipper. "Tastes better when you're hungry."

Boat food is eaten quickly and with desperation—the hunger of the body as well as of the mind. Fishing is often boring, and food offers an interesting distraction for the senses. We are hungry all the time, burning calories at a colossal rate for people who never walk more than a few steps at once. We eat several times a day when we're working long hours—sandwiches, quick cups of noodles, fistfuls of crackers crammed in between sets. My mom once made an enormous triple batch of chocolate chip cookie dough; we were working steadily, and she was pinched for time and planning to bake them later in the day. Deckhands stumbled in and out of the cabin, chewing furtively on deck, and by the time she got back inside, the entire bowl of dough had disappeared before a single cookie could be baked. She was so angry, she cried.

The rare meals in which we sat at the galley table to eat were often still a race—we shoveled food onto our plates and off again, into our mouths, before it was time to get back on deck or before another deckhand ate it all, a competition for quantity in the manner of families with lots of siblings. Determined not to be the runt, I learned to inhale my food to ensure my portion, a habit I've carried with me since. While others linger over dinner party salads and small talk and have taken what appears to be scant polite bites of the meal, I'll look down and find my plate already scraped clean, my cutlery signaling completion at the angle of ten and four o'clock. More than one raised eyebrow has suggested that perhaps I was afraid my food was going to escape?

I guess I am.

There is a deep anxiety attached to the experience of hunger or loss of food. Conversely, the comfort it affords can be rich and layered—a well-timed bar of chocolate floods the body with chemistry that brings on cellular quietude, a sense of peace from the inside out; endorphins curl thick and dreamlike and dark sweetness flows across the tongue. Sometimes I received care packages from friends in the Lower 48, often including magazines and candy. I tried to hide these things in my bunk to avoid having them stolen by crewmates, their irreplaceable value far more precious than money in the limited economy of the boat. Finding my sleeping bag and pillowcase ransacked was a violation of the highest order—like having care itself taken from me. I learned to cut secret stashes of chocolate into smaller pieces and hide them separately to ensure better chances of survival and return, like a squirrel banking nuts for the winter. I

engaged in deep psy-ops and camouflage, pretending to have nothing, never gloating, tucking parcels of Snickers wrapped in paper
into tampon boxes and inside stashes of dry woolen socks.

I watched crew members get sentimental about their food too.
Some were young, barely men, my mom standing in for their own
comfort figures of the past, the food standing in for the nostalgic
starches of their childhoods.

One deckhand sighed wistfully and said, without irony, "These
potatoes are so good. They're even better than prison mashed potatoes," which became our family's insider compliment for any meal.

I watched how crew reacted to the food my mom produced, and
I learned how simply a person's needs can be met, how a good meal
can bring a sense of collectivity and shared enjoyment, how offering
a well-timed snack or hot drink can make someone feel seen or loved
better than any words.

Sailors used to use knotted rope trailing the stern as an indicator of
their vessel's speed. My indicator of a good day was watching the
peanut shells float past. If the weather was clear, all the better—but
when the water was reasonably calm and we were looking for fish,
music would float down from the wheelhouse, and a breeze of peanut husks would tumble from the upper window, setting adrift a tiny
flotilla of shells.

On these days, I would scamper up the side of the boat, my
rubber boots sure on the gritty paint. I'd hook a wrist into the railing
beneath the wheelhouse, and there would be my dad, one elbow
casually propped out the window and his beard past the sill, eyes
trained on the water. With one hand, he'd make effortless adjust-
ments to our course or throttle. With the other, he'd pull handfuls
of salted peanuts from the bag in his lap, cracking them one at a
time with his mouth and tossing the shells out the window, bluegrass

drowning out the radio chatter. The process of selecting, shelling, of popping something small into the mouth is difficult to do while angry. Peanuts always meant he was in a good mood.

I would lean away from the cabin at an angle, my hand on the railing, my head out over the waves like a starboard figurehead. A fist would appear above my face, and I'd accept my own handful of peanuts and watch for jumpers with him, as if we were at a sporting event together on a sunny day. I loved the double saltiness—the dried seawater turned to crust on the railing and coming off onto my hands as powder, the same powdery salt clinging to the shells. Peanuts were a dad thing, not for general consumption—he even stored them in the wheelhouse in one of the cubbies no one else touched. They were his happy, thinking snack, and getting to share them made me feel important. It was also a way to leave the deck and carve out a tiny bit of space for myself, my own little gap of infinite, hanging off the side of the boat.

Close quarters for prolonged periods of time can be indistinguishable from confinement in many ways. Small irritations become magnified. Unlike marriages, where the fight over the way one loads the dishwasher is actually about something else, on a boat, the fight really can be about the way one chews their meat. Similar to prison, I imagine, these tiny offenses gain new importance in the context of the cabin. We had a skiffman once who automatically slathered his meat in condiments, regardless of preparation. On a rare steak night, his meat disappeared beneath a half inch of ketchup, and my father almost fired him on the spot. I saw an argument nearly come to blows over whose corn cob was cleaner after the kernels had been gnawed off. One woman held her fork like an ice pick to stab into any hand that reached near seconds or thirds that she had her eyes on. After a certain point, my dad stopped eating in the galley altogether, choosing to take his meals in the wheelhouse instead, saying he'd spent enough of his life eating with the crew.

There is also the unwanted intimacy of knowing every individual's private food habits—who smears butter across the top of a muffin and who splits it instead. Who puts salt into their palm before dumping it onto their food. Who sighs and closes their eyes as they chew. One always liked fish cooked whole and would eat the eyeballs first. Another was concerned he wasn't "getting his money's worth" with the amount taken from his share for fuel and food, so he took to tabulating ingredients and estimating their real market value. When he felt shorted, he would drink sweetened condensed milk straight from the can to make up the difference, as it was the highest dollar value per ounce he could find.

Don wears a red Mustang survival suit and a bandana tied around his head, every day. Every day he methodically removes a dozen Lipton or Red Rose tea bags from their paper wrappers, tugging the strings together. I watch the pile of little envelopes grow on the rubber mesh of the galley table. He ties the dozen strings together in a single knot and stuffs the tea bags into a half-gallon clear plastic jug that's long ago turned a leathery brown. Every day, he pours boiling water over the teabags and carries the jug out to the skiff with him, whistling something classical but obscure—never Mozart, possibly Liszt or Brahms. Every day, he refills it at least once.

"That shit'll tan yer insides," my dad growls, elbowing Don in the ribs. They grew up together and share a sense of humor.

Don retorts with something about baseball mitts and ball sacs, something I miss. I'm never quite sure what he means.

When we're anchored up, he often quizzes me on things he thinks I'm supposed to know: the capital of Argentina, the name of the famous aria from *Madame Butterfly*, the main ingredient in beer. I wonder why a man with such a gift for trivia likes to spend his summers in a skiff. My mom explains that he's a teacher the rest of the year.

I don't really care if Don tans his insides; he likes tea, and that seems fine to me. I do get disappointed when he drinks Lipton, though. In every box of Red Rose is a small animal figurine—an owl, a lion, a bear. They're all coated in a thick pastel glaze that obscures their details but makes them shiny and pleasantly smooth to the touch. Sometimes he shares these animals with me, a precious gesture I try hard to earn. They are silly as objects, lazily mass produced, hardly a treasure. But Don is like an uncle to me; I want to get his questions right. I see the importance he places on the tea, its ritual value for him—the animals are like extensions of this, little tea totems, powerful pieces of trade in our tiny symbolic world. A small menagerie takes the form of a tumbled altar, crammed alongside a Japanese wooden egg box stuffed with cassette tapes on a galley shelf.

~

Food also engenders a small and compassionate economy of barter—sharing becomes a form of camaraderie and care, sometimes among strangers.

I fell in love for a day with a young woman on a tender who leaned across the gap between our two boats and, over the slosh of the water between us, handed me a plate of chocolate chip cookies still warm from the oven. It was as if all human kindness had condensed into that paper plate, and I received it, holding my breath.

The *Balaena* with its soft-serve ice cream machine in the galley made it the gold standard in tenders. We would fight over who got to go aboard and maybe return with a cone.

Sometimes other crews would offer salmon or weed for bread, treats, other kinds of fish, recipes for barbecue sauce, or the offspring of a hundred-year-old sourdough starter handed down from someone's prospector great-grandfather, lovingly cradled in a small glass jar. It was immediate, and it was what we had to offer.

~

The Alutiiq village of Larsen Bay was home to an old woman who lived with her family and half a dozen dogs. Her house was out on stilts on the edge of the water, her face wizened and flat, her laugh smoky and loud from her belly. She had a secret that she had received from her grandmother, and she from her mother before her— she knew the trick to making the perfect smoked fish. She never revealed her recipe or her process, but dense fragrance plumed about the smoker hut next to her home, and the weathered gray boards were black at the edges from years of burnt sugar and browned scales. The arrangement was, we'd give her two salmon and get one back, turned to candy—dense and alchemically transformed. It was a deep magic she worked on that fish, sticky, chewy, full of sweet wood and oil and smoke. It was as if earth and sea and sky came together into one rose-colored crystal to be gnawed from the tough salmon skin.

13

Letter

Dear Sir —
Though I have never seen the ocean, I think I would
bring good karma to your ship.

Dear Skipper —
Me and Johnny have been working at the Barrel O' Fun,
so I got good experience working with others. My
grandpa used to take me fishing up in the lakes, so I
know my way around a fish.

Attention: Skipper
I hear there's a lot of money to be made fishing in
Alaska, and all I can say is, I'm in!

WHEN THE BOOK was published that explained how lucrative salmon
fishing was in the 1980s, it offered a recommendation: write letters
to highliner skippers in advance of the season to secure a place on
their crew. It also provided a list of skippers' names and addresses,
which included nearly everyone in the fleet, with the exception of
the author. My parents received a flood of hopeful, clueless missives for years after the book came out—dreamy, earnest, bizarre
letters from landlocked readers, all hoping to make a fortune in
the course of a few months' work. In retrospect, my folks wish they
had saved them all, a time capsule representing a little slice of an
era. The senders' often misguided and even hilarious attempts at
self-promotion represented a spectrum of backgrounds, yet they
also illustrated a deep and widespread longing for adventure beyond the options their own lives offered. They were hungry for
something intangible, a fantasy that fishing in Alaska put within

reach. My parents had both gone north for much the same reasons when they were younger.

Letters have always been related to treasure-seeking in Alaska. Much of the pressure to improve the mail delivery system in the Far North came from the huge influx of post sent to those prospectors who came to Alaska during the gold rush. Mail traveled by dog sled along the Yukon River and Iditarod Trail; dogs could only handle so much weight, particularly during the winter, and people often waited months for word from home.

For us, any letter or package that made its way to our hands on the fishing grounds was brought by a tender, after having arrived at the cannery via bush plane, airplane, truck, and carrier, all the way from the Lower 48. I like to imagine the number of hands and piles our mail passed through on its journey, bundles of bills and notes and cards, magazines and care packages, all traveling in the pockets, bags, gloves, cubbies, cargo holds of strangers, a transmission of the precious through trust.

Sometimes a letter would take weeks. Friends would often send newspapers, knowing the scarcity of fresh reading material on the boat. It wasn't about the news—the content was long stale by the time it arrived. Even the daily goings-on and bits of gossip and updates they shared had become past tense by the time our eyes held them. The important thing was just in the sharing, the reminding one another, "I'm still here. This other life is still here." Their handwriting reminded me that real people loved and missed us; it gave tangible evidence of a world that wasn't damp or salt crusted, that didn't smell of fish, or rumble incessantly, or rock and vibrate and hum.

Being on the boat is a very isolating experience—*isol* from "island," another small space surrounded by water. It is a microsociety of five people with a chief and inhabitants, each with our own social niches to fill. It is unlike anywhere else; so many of the qualities we embody elsewhere are invisible, unused. It can sometimes be hard to remember exactly who we are when we are not a deckhand, who else we have been besides the one who stacks the corks, or the one who pitches fish the slowest. Some remind themselves with music, by playing guitar or flute or radio. Some ramble on in mini lectures about philosophy or forestry or NASCAR. Still others sketch, or knit, or tell stories about the fruit trees growing in their yards back home. I drew pictures and wrote letters of my own.

This split personality was hard when I was younger. It was often jarring, hearing news from home and realizing that life went on without me. Plus, the different indicators of success or identity from one world to the next were so divergent, so irrelevant to one another: nobody on the boat cared about what song lyrics I'd memorized or what hand clap games I knew. Nobody on the playground down south could tell the difference between a humpie and a king.

As a teen, I'd sit on the soft web pile in my damp raingear, several days distant from any kind of shower and having forgotten to look in a mirror for days, reading a note from a friend back home. I would feel a sharp lance of self-consciousness, a reminder that there were people elsewhere curling their bangs, applying cologne, being concerned about colors that matched. The gulf between us would widen. What difference do colors make when they're under yellow raingear? My hair was tucked under a handkerchief, stuffed beneath a gurry-stained cap. Even if I did clean myself up, who would be there to notice besides the rest of the crew? There is a deep ease to living filthy, to being freed from the expectation of looking good and being clean. Yet I would catch myself going inside to carefully braid my hair again, hacking at it with a brush to remove the glittering fish scales that clung or the salt that held the ends in thick points, like a fistful of paint brushes.

As I grew older and learned to fill in the various roles my life offered, I found bits of self to overlap and stayed connected to friends back home by building these small bridges inside myself. I wrote them letters in return that let me use any voice I wanted, and I discovered that the letter voice was the same no matter where I was. I talked about the surface of the water, the way the sky looked, and strange things that had come up in the net. It made a space for my boat self to project elsewhere and be reflected back by my friends, all people who would appreciate such things. They noticed the sky where they were too. They liked to poke weird ocean things with a stick. I clung to the idea that we would be "normal" together again—watch movies, stretch our legs over longs walks, drink coffee in a coffeeshop—all things that were out of reach for me on the boat. I learned that we persist across great distances and impossible shifts in focus, that we are flexible and adaptive, and there is space within us for many, many lives.

~

Miss is a word root from Latin, meaning "to send." Missile, missive, mission. Things are sent with purpose. If letters are about the slow elasticity of human connection, packages are about the sweetness of attention to detail. Care packages were like gold. The arrival of a care package was like a visitation from royalty: space was cleared, time was set aside so as to give it undivided attention. I would hoard it, shake it, and press my ear to its sides. I would run my hands over its surfaces, enjoying the way my name looked in another's scrawl. I would make myself wait until the last possible instant, when I could no longer stand the anticipation, and then tear it open, pulling out each bit of wrapping or candy or slip of paper as if it were treasure.

Sometimes their contents were well-meaning but useless—a lover once sent me three packets of bubble bath, thinking I could use them to relax. I laughed, wondering if there was a bathtub for fifty miles. They smelled nice, so I poured them into a bowl of hot water and soaked my feet, an extravagance of both time and scent, as my feet immediately returned to the soggy, rancid boots where they lived.

Other times packages were perfect examples of the simplest gestures being the deepest form of care: fancy cocoa mix, magazines, a handmade bandana, a delicious tropical lip balm. Finding the perfect small item that can encapsulate luxury, ease, and escapism—and be sent through a postal system that will no doubt leave it battered, ragged, and soaked—is a true art form. My friends revealed new facets of their creativity to me through the things they decided to send.

One woman sent handmade cartoons she'd painstakingly colored with pencils and wrapped around boxes of tampons and incense that smelled like her hair.

A friend on another boat sent sheaves of charcoal sketches of beachcombed bones he made during wheelwatch, along with a grenade of fancy whiskey he'd no doubt been saving for himself and a single cigar. He asked me to share them with my mom because he wanted to imagine us smoking together.

Another deckhand from a different cannery used pastels to recreate a scene from a book we both loved—on the inside of a brown grocery bag, the only clean paper he could find.

I received a box of petals from a friend in Oregon. No note, no other wrapping—just a small cardboard box, taped round and round that, when split open with a fishing knife, poured forth a small swell of wilted purple blossoms. I had opened it on deck, and the breeze caught them and scattered them across the net and into the wake behind us.

Sometimes there were love letters. I would memorize these, hearing their voice in my head as I ran my eyes over the shapes of their handwriting, over and over again. Knowing that their fingertips had been in such close proximity to the very page I now held rendered the paper a transportive magic, a talisman that brought them somehow closer to my skin. I would breathe these pages in, hoping for more than just the scent of ink, some trace of their animal chemistry that would raise the hair on my neck. If I found it, I would wear it out with repetition, bury my receptors with the same signal, over and over, trying to keep the pheromonal ghost of them close. And then I would sit down to write in return, investing the paper with every bit of myself I could, hoping the intention behind my words was as loud as it felt in my chest.

This patient form of communication helps underscore the fantasy and projection of courtship. Instead of immediate swipes and texts, there were long stretches of imagination, of longing to fill in the gaps. Much was built and dreamed of in those periods of waiting between one letter and the next; the briefest of words gained paragraphs of meaning through hope and anticipation. When they said they "miss me," did they mean they *miss* me? Or did they just miss me? When they said they loved what I wrote, did they mean *love*? The investment of attention added weight and consequence.

It also made letters containing breakups that much more surreal—the lag time in reality, the mismatch of narratives, the realization that one had been dreaming alone for some time. When things ended by post, the news often arrived too late. I learned about the end of one relationship when a friend casually complained about a person she was sleeping with. I read it three times, waiting for the raw shock to wear off, since the person she mentioned was my own boyfriend—I'd thought. His letter came two weeks after, having been held up somewhere along the way.

There was a tacit period of silence after we all retrieved mail from the office at the cannery. We left each other alone to catch up on news, to light up and crack apart, depending on the messages. These mirrors of ourselves that arrived in paper form were precious, and we didn't need to share all our faces with each other. We gave each other time to crawl back into our fishing personae if we'd strayed too far into our other selves.

Mail was often followed by collect calls. Lines formed along the planks leading up to the cannery telephones during closures. The walls of the booths were tattooed with tiny letters, missives with no destination but out—scribbles, rude jokes, numbers to be remembered. Heartbreak was scrawled with a penknife into the beaten wood.

I'll love you forever.

Why GINA WHY

i want to come home.

14

Glove

THERE IS A SMALL BIN made of an old wooden egg box lashed near the hydraulic controls. It is filled with a tumble of tools, all made to extend what the hands can do: long plastic needles for mending gear, sharp knives in cardboard sheaths, cylinders of twine, and gloves. It is clear at a glance which gloves are which, what they're for, whose are whose. My mom sometimes draws smiley faces on the backs of hers. A deckhand carefully labels *L* and *R* in magic marker, only half in jest. Some have been marked to look like kindergarten Thanksgiving turkeys; still others have their owner's names printed inside the cuffs in block letters.

I wear heavy orange gloves as I stack the leads, thick protection and friction for my fingers to grip the purse line. Water slides down my arms and slips into the space between the glove and my wrist, tiny serpents of cold against my skin. I dry the gloves by the stove in the evenings with the sleeves rolled back—having toasty gloves to slip on first thing in the morning is almost as good as fresh socks, though once on deck, the warmth lasts half as long.

My mom's thin yellow gloves are papery and soft. She stacks the web, huge cascades of dark net tumbling from the block overhead, forming a wall between the deckhands and the rest of the deck. The web billows into our faces in a stiff wind. It rains salt water and drops kelp and gilled fish and jellies and lumps of clay with unceremonious thumps. The web sometimes snags and runs back upward when the net slips or the gear strains. When this happens, we have to pull with all our weight.

"What's the point of wearing dishwashing gloves when your hands get soaked anyway?" I asked once. My mom pointed up at the massive hydraulic block shackled overhead, its inexorable turn like a millstone dangling above us.

"If my hand gets caught, I hope it rips off the glove and not my fingers," she said.

~

During downtime, people look at their hands. Fingers and palms collect esoteric patterns of injury, like ogham writing cut into branches or stones, telling stories of what has transpired there. The crew like to recount them one by one, sharing particularly gruesome ones with pride. "Comparing owies," my folks call it, grown men holding bruises and cuts next to each other's like schoolboys showing off Band-Aids. One has electrical tape holding a finger closed; another got fish slime in a deep cut and it's showing all the puffy, angry signs of infection.

I use my thumbnail to peel an iridescent scale from the bone of my wrist and pretend I have begun my final transformation into mermaid.

~

There are two other types of gloves in the box. Both are for pitching fish, but people have their own tastes when it comes to which work best. There are white cloth gloves that have been crisscrossed with rubber, like the drizzle across a fancy cookie. One skiffman likes to wear these to pitch fish because he can feel through them. They are flexible and fast and allow his fingers to move naturally. His grip is strong, and he only needs that slight bit of extra tack to hold the girth of a fish in each hand with ease.

One of these gloves falls into the hold and I haul it out from behind a bin panel. It is as if the entire thing has begun to melt; it runs with a stream of salmon gurry, a thin, pink syrup made of salt and fear and mucus. I wring it out and toss it onto the deck. It lands with a wet *splock*, like the carcass of a pale, ruined cephalopod. I step on an edge and blast it with the deck hose. When I wring it out again, it remains gooey and slick. I hate these gloves.

The kind I use to pitch look like part of a cheap monster costume. They're rich crustacean red and are studded all over with tiny angled chips of hard rubber, like they've been dipped in tar and broken glass and then vulcanized. They are stiff and far too wide for my hands—when I put them on, I bend my fingers as if only jointed at the edge of the palm, my hands little better than wide pincers. But the jagged surface grips fish well, and they let me toss the slick silver corpses of salmon at any angle, without reaching for the tail or slowing my pace. It feels like wearing bionic hands, stronger than my own.

When I was in college, I skipped fishing one summer to study in Germany. I received a letter there that puzzled me—the return address said it was from my mother, but the handwriting looked nothing like her familiar script. It had the quavering, palsied cursive of someone half again her age. The letters on the envelope were formed in cautious loops, as if their author had had to concentrate very hard to produce the correct shapes.

Dear Sweetie –

she began,

I want you to know that I'm fine.

Which, of course, meant that she was not. I braced myself for the rest, feeling acutely the distance between Berlin and Kodiak Island.

The letter went on to explain that they had been fishing in a heavy chop. The set had ended, and she and the other deckhand had lifted the hatch cover and were pitching fish from the deck into the hold as fast as they could, each bracing against the swell with one hand. The boat turned sharply to set again, and the hatch cover had slid and slammed sideways, trapping her free hand between it and the side of the hold.

I held up my hand and my glove was filling with blood, the letter continued.

The other guys on deck helped me when they saw my fingers pointing the wrong directions. They escorted me up to the wheelhouse, and your dad was wondering where the hell the crew was—he was ready to make another set.

"I think I've done something really bad," I said to him.

The fingers of the glove were ballooning as if attached to a faucet. She was afraid to take it off, for fear her own fingers had been severed from her hand. The others began to peel the glove away and saw bits of mashed flesh mingled with the blood in the cotton lining. She was in shock.

Most owies on the boat are fixed with meat tenderizer or tape, but it was clear that she needed more than the first-aid kit under the sink. They put out a call for help; a deckhand kept her arm elevated, and another boat sent pain meds over in a skiff. The swell made a water landing dangerous, but my dad radioed into town and lied about the weather to get a bush pilot to fly out. The pilot was furious when he realized the landing conditions, and the plane busted two pontoon struts before finally lurching again into the air like a clumsy seabird, but he got her to town and to the emergency room.

At the hospital, her hand was stitched back together, the fingers still attached but crushed, all four fingers broken. The threat of infection or swelling damage meant she had to stay clean and quiet for some time, so she stayed with a friend in Kodiak for a few weeks, drinking tea, reading books, writing me letters with her left hand—carefully forming the words, recovery slowly smoothing the shakes from her pen.

From across the world, I watched the progress of her healing, using her handwriting as a barometer. As she was able to shift the pen back to her right, the writing again became tentative and tender, but the letters grew more confident and robust as the pain receded and other sensations and control returned to her hand. She told me that the doctors said the glove had probably saved her, cushioning the blow so the hatch didn't cut through the bones. It wasn't much, but it served its purpose. By winter, her handwriting was back to normal.

15

Radio

I.

"YOUR SON HAS A POWERFUL HEARTBEAT," the doctors had told my mother before she headed north to Alaska. She and my father had selected a strong, traditional German name for their little boy: Hans Gustav. She was still smallish in the belly; in her raingear, no one could tell she was pregnant, and she wasn't on deck for long. She had just finished her second trimester when she left the boat for the summer in July.

She spent an uncomfortable night at a friend's place in Kodiak, plagued by minor cramps, and then flew south to Pullman, Washington, where she planned to visit her mother briefly before heading back to the Midwest to wait out the last hot, restless months before my due date in early October. Once in Pullman, what she thought was a gas pain turned out to be early contractions, which grew more frequent and severe until she was rushed to the hospital. The doctors did everything they could to quell the waves beginning inside of her, and they battled for long hours to stop the labor. I was, however, insistent. I was delivered on July 22 at Pullman Regional Hospital, nine and a half weeks prematurely.

This was long before cell phones. To share the news with my father, my mom had to place a call through the hospital switchboard to an operator, who then connected to the Harbormaster's office in Kodiak; the Harbormaster radioed the cannery, which sent the dispatch out to the fishing grounds. The message of my birth was then bounced from boat to boat via VHF until my father finally received the news, probably in a quick pause between sets.

"I was the last in the fleet to know!" he shakes his head and palms his brow in disbelief every time he tells the story.

Onlookers report I was a red, fuzzy lizard—my weight dropped to three and a half pounds, and I was placed in an incubator to finish the cooking process for a handful of weeks. I wasn't done yet, and no one was allowed to touch me until I was.

I try to imagine what that must have been like for my mother, alone but for her mom, no friends, no partner—and unable to hold her miniature newborn, who lay cradled in a plastic box, filled with tubes. Furthermore, though my heart was proving as strong as promised, Hans Gustav no longer seemed a good fit. Having been assured of a son, my parents had no girl names picked out. What was she to do?

It took weeks of shuttling lists back and forth via post and costly ship-to-shore calls through the radio to arrive at a few common favorite girl names. Meanwhile, Baby X, as I was known in the hospital records, continued to grow, my little heartbeat pinging with reassuring cadence on the monitors. As I grew, the radio served as the only link between my mother and the boat, the thin transmission of voice and the static crackle making it more like communing with a spirit than with a hot-blooded human. Wires and wavelengths were the only ways my family could connect. At last, they chose the name Lara Lee.

II.

Once I was on the boat, radio continued to be the link that led back to dry land. Every evening, we all paused what we were doing at 6:00 to listen to Peggy Dyson give the weather, like a Norman Rockwell family crowded around a television set.

"Hello, all mariners," every broadcast began, "this is WBH29 Kodiak." Her voice would read out each region with its unique microclimates and meteorological circumstances—wind speeds, tides, the heights of the waves. We had to listen closely for our location; we didn't want to miss it, especially if it felt like the weather was about to take a turn for the worse. It was like at home the rest of the year—I was never allowed to talk during Johnny Carson's monologue. Nobody spoke when Peggy read the weather.

"... [unclear] 15 knots ... [unclear] ... four-foot seas ... Southeast ..."

Sometimes the signal on the side band was weak or flattened by interference; we often had to lean in to hear her clearly. I remember watching my dad squint as if her voice were tiny letters that would snap into focus if only he could narrow the field of vision a bit more. She always sounded calm, blurred by static, and distinctly nasal. Her litany transmitted over the miles seemed almost mechanically generated, like a gentle mariner robot droning through a pipe.

"Gale warning," we would mimic any time the weather was bad, humming the cautionary phrase through our noses, "gale warning."

Radio was also the primary way news spread to the fleet. Like long-haul truckers, small shorthand developed between boats for warning that the Coasties were nearby, in case anyone had drugs on board. Radio brought news of celebrity deaths from the mainland, of political developments, and important sports scores. Don had a shortwave radio in his bunk, which brought sounds from across the Bering Strait. Unfamiliar voices and cadences drifted out from his den in the fo'c'sle, the mysterious sounds of Radio Moscow or music I had never heard before. Sometimes the BBC crackled through, and Don would explain how the radio waves bounced off the atmosphere and landed within range, making the world seem like a cacophony of invisible voices chattering at all angles across oceans of silence.

III.

Radio was also used to keep information hidden. There were secret codes for fish, ways to share how big one's last set was only to a chosen few. Skippers and skiffmen used encrypted channels, insider language, and even hand signals to prevent other boats from knowing how well (or how poorly) things were going. Combines and friends let one another in on hot spots and dead zones, encouraging allies to join them in riches but not to come running, to avoid making it look like they'd been summoned down the beach.

Even the alphabetic brevity code, formally known as the International Radiotelephony Spelling Alphabet, was used to identify boats and call signals. Like the twenty-four-hour clock, which spared us having to say AM or PM, the code was a standard holdover from the military, intended to disambiguate sounds over the radio, the subtleties of English fricatives and nasals often lost at the edges of the transmitted frequency. I found, though, that it also served a dual purpose of creating an insider/outsider knowledge set. It was one of the many means of marking a deckhand as green or seasoned—whether they knew the alphabet substitutions by heart.

For a long time, our call sign was WAD 8603, and Whiskey-Alfa-Delta became a poem I knew like a nursery rhyme. When I was a child, the words formed automatic associations with the letters for me—much like kindergarten posters or sets of blocks irreversibly link A with apple or B with ball, the images of Alfa-Bravo-Charlie-Delta scrolled past in my head like pictures on a wheel. I disliked how "Mike" was followed by "November," as if the creators had no sense of rhythm at all, but I loved the sequence of "Oscar-Papa-Quebec-Romeo," the flare of the colors that the sounds held for me reflected back in the shapes of the images. Ivory and black Oscar slid into the violet of Papa and the rich purple-green fold of Quebec, ending with a royal-black-copper structure in Romeo. It made these things easy to remember, and I felt like knowing them was proof of some small and esoteric initiation—it showed in a tiny way that I belonged.

I learned a lot by listening to men talk on the radio. A large proportion of what I learned consisted of off-color jokes and a dizzying range of profanity, but I also learned ways of thinking. Sometimes men would share stories as they stared back at their nets, waiting for the fish to swim in. Sometimes they made things up. I could tell when they were lonely, when they were angry, when they were trying to impress one another. Sometimes they talked out their strategies in an offhand way, as if they just wanted their thinking to be recognized. Other times, they muttered gruff monosyllables, directions, clipped responses to jibes. This was part of how they built their hierarchies, their trusts. It was a small club, and listening in was one of the only ways I could ever be a part of it.

IV.

One summer, I flew up a little later in the season to meet my parents on the boat. I had already made the long trek to Alaska, and once I got to Kodiak, the final leg of the journey remained. Normally I would have flown out to the cannery in Larsen Bay and met them there, but they were on hot fish and the weather was nasty, so I either had to camp out for a few days or fly directly to the fishing grounds in what is known as a "puddle jumper"; I chose to head straight to the boat.

The rain felt like diagonal nails hammering into me as I lugged my gear down the boardwalk. A bush pilot with a reckless grin and a springy walk met me, taking my duffle bag off my shoulder.

"You must be Lara Lee," he said. "Hang tight—it's gonna be exciting."

I swallowed a spike of anxiety at this—pontoon planes are always exciting, but I felt more at ease when the pilots didn't think so. He completed my thought, adding, "We should have the place to ourselves," meaning the sky, I supposed. "I don't think anybody else is going to chance this." My nervousness must have showed, because his grin softened to a smile that was clearly intended to invoke confidence. "Don't worry," he said. "We'll get you there."

Once my gear was stowed, he showed me how to attach the seat harness, which was a little more complicated than the standard clip-and-pulls from the commercial airlines that had gotten me this far.

He handed me an enormous set of headphones and pantomimed putting them on, which I did, adjusting the small microphone in front of my mouth that would allow us to communicate over the noise of the engines on our own private frequency. After a quick, practiced check of the instrument panels and some brief exchanges with local air traffic control, we were taxiing through the water, preparing for takeoff.

The sound in a small plane is enormous. Even with the headphones on, the roar made my teeth ache, and every cell in my body felt jostled apart by the vibration. As the plane gained speed, I had the sensation of sinking rather than flying—there was no runway to push against, so the plane buried its hindquarters in the water, at once tilting us upward at an angle and dragging back on our bodies in a way that reminded me of a rocket launch, as if we were trying to reach escape velocity and make it to the moon rather than simply hop up into the air. Once we were aloft, though, the sensation was more familiar, except that we were far lower than I was accustomed to, and I was pretty sure he banked directly over an outcropping of rocks just to test my nerves. I was too enraptured by the view to care.

We were in what is known as a two-seater spotter plane—herring fisheries, especially, often consist of a collaboration between a boat and a pilot, known as a spotter. For fish that don't jump, it can be hard to see large schools from the surface of the water, but they form clear dark patches from high above that can be easily spotted from the air. To help with viewing, the windows in the cabin are curved sharply outward, like bubbles, so both passenger and pilot can lean completely out past the edge of the plane and look straight down.

We were flying close over the land at first. The forest raced beneath us like a field of dark pinnacles, the green of the treetops feeling like they were only a hair's breadth beneath the landing gear. Clearings popped open and then vanished. Small streams whipped snakelike and silver, glinting and disappearing into the trees.

The radio buzzed in my headphones, and I turned to look at the pilot. I shook my head. He adjusted his mic and tried again, pointing. I followed his gesture and saw a bear running below us. "Ain't that something?" I heard through the static and engine noise. We met each other's eyes and grinned.

I watched an eagle race away from us at an angle. At that moment, we reached the end of the woods, and the ground burst away from us as if we had finally taken flight, become birdlike ourselves, the cliffside plummeting downward and the snarl of gray water churning into whitecaps below. I caught my breath and leaned out as far as I could, bracing against the turbulence in the air and staring into the leaden surface of the waves. Tide rips and currents were hard to see in the chop, but there were still clear, dark patches and shadows describing the motion happening far beneath the surface.

As we made our way down the coastline, I watched the forms of the land rearrange until they clicked into familiar shapes, the crags of capes and the parabolic swoops of hillsides that our nautical charts were meant to describe. Though the maps we used gave us details of the deeps—shoals and shallows and channels for safe passage— the landmasses were described in dull washes of color with pinpoint landmarks, pale ghosts of the rich landscape that fell away before me with its small stones and shifting thickets of driftwood, the wildflowers and the stony green shrouded in fog.

As we bounced and white-knuckled our way to the fishing grounds, I began to see the tiny shapes of the fleet: the boats like models, making their way around round little nets; the tender waiting quietly at anchor in the bay. The pilot was already talking with our boat on another channel.

Landing on the water was akin to landing in a quarry, or on a minefield studded with moguls. As we slammed down and decelerated across the surface of the waves, I found myself again grateful for the harness that held me in place. We pitched and lurched, the wind pushing us like a sail. I unclenched my jaw only to realize we now had to tie up in this weather. I recognized the familiar outline of the boat; we taxied to a stop until we were close enough that I could read *Lara Lee* on the stern, bobbing in the swell. The pilot hopped out onto the landing gear, tossing the painter to my dad, who was beaming. The crew grabbed my bags, and I timed my jump, clambered over the bulwarks and across the wet bulk of the net, the scent of salt and diesel, the sweet tang of fish and blood flooding me, more familiar than freshly baked bread. My parents were there, and we were all smiling. They both held me tight at once. Wherever we were, I was home.

16

Wake

I.

THE FIRST SOUND I HEAR every morning at four o'clock is the sound of the skipper putting on his boots. I know this sound because it reminds me that I was in such a hurry to get into my bunk at one o'clock this morning, after I got done pitching mixed fish for three hours and then fixing that tear in the bag from the snag the skiffman dragged us over the top of and then washing the dishes from dinner, that I forgot to take my own boots off, and so I've been sleeping on top of my rank sleeping bag in damp sweatpants and a tank top, with my wet feet moldering inside the godforsaken confines of my Xtra Tuffs.

Then I hear footsteps, and I think to yourself, "Maybe he's just taking a leak." I try to salvage another precious eighteen seconds of sleep before the fantasy is shattered. I have spent the entire luxurious three hours of rack time dreaming that I was pitching fish, so in my mind, I really haven't slept at all.

This is why I go back to sleep in the twelve seconds it takes the skipper to reach topside. But then there's the squeal. To start a diesel engine, you first have to turn the key on for several ear-splitting seconds as it readies. It squeals, rumbles, and finally chuffs like a locomotive picking up speed. This is when the waking game really starts.

The game is pretty simple: the first deckhand out of the sack to pull the anchor wins the bad-ass award. It means you are a superior worker. It means you are the strongest, smartest, most keen-eyed, and highest-paid deck monkey of them all. You get bragging rights. If you win all the time, you get to guilt other deckhands into doing things for you: "I pulled the pick again. You get to . . ." pump the bilge by hand, clean out the shitter, plunge—whatever.

It also means that, in my hustle, I trip on the step heading out of the galley because someone forgot to close the lid on the glove cubby. It means that I am staggering out onto the deck in the dark, only to find that I didn't grab a sweatshirt because I wasn't going to lose the race and eat shit like I did the last three mornings, so now my bleary eyes are being pelted with the rain that has already been whittled into stinging bullets by the time it's fallen from the sky and been blown sideways by the thirty-five-knot winds that have picked up since we dropped anchor mere hours ago.

I cling to the railing as I run up the side to the bow, and when the skipper gives the signal, I start the hydraulic winch heaving the cable up, deftly knocking it into place along the spool so it doesn't grab or kink on its way out next time. Then the cable turns to chain, and I realize there is so much goddamn kelp on the pick itself that it won't come all the way up, so I have to scamper back to the gear closet and grab my knife and run back to the bow so I can lean way out over the edge and hack at the kelp ball, with nothing but slippery seaweed and a slimy chain to hold onto. Then I finally heave the damn thing onto the mount on the prow and kill the winch, remembering to tie a safety line onto the chain with a quick-release knot. I know how to do this because I am the bad-ass, the superior worker. I am the A-1 deck monkey. And then I haul my now freezing, soaking wet ass back into the galley where I find that someone else has already started the coffee going, and I get to snag three more minutes of sleep before we hit the fishing grounds. I take my boots off, change my socks, and hit the rack hard. I win.

II.

Enter into any channel and you'll see a sign posted, "5mph—No wake." The wake is the footprint of the passing boat, the frothing trail it carves behind it, with crests curling off at angles and churned up water between. When we traveled, I would often spend hours staring back behind us at our wake. Sometimes the wake would glow green with bioluminescent algae in the dusk. Sometimes the seas would be so rough, the wake would get lost as the waves leapt and folded up and in on themselves. If the sea were calm, it left a scar on the surface that would last for as long as I could watch it before it disappeared into the optical tricks of waterlight. Sometimes I thought of it as slicing the skin of a vast, beautiful animal, and I felt ashamed.

The water tells me it is alive because it becomes so many other things. The metaphors are endless: The ocean as cornucopia, as we haul an enormous bag of fish over the side. The ocean as a voluptuous woman, when I see its swells and heaves and everything is hips and breasts and asses and tides, pulled about by the moon. The ocean as beast, all-powerful and unable to be reasoned with, smashing everything in its path. The ocean as dangerous magic, prompting superstition and tattoos and rituals for safe passage. The ocean as desert, flat and endless, undrinkable, burning with salt, the sun beating down. The ocean as wine. As ink. As a horse, bucking and wild.

When the ocean is calm, the surface becomes glassy and reflective. It turns the color of mercury and makes interlocking shapes of gray and black and silver, looping ovals that whorl in and out of each other, like shadows boiling. This is something that cannot be seen from the shore because the waves break the surface and destroy the tension and the symmetry. It is beautiful, dark yet full of color. I used to wonder whether that beauty is meant to mesmerize, to make death painless. Sometimes I would stare out onto the surface of the ocean and wonder if that was what was happening to me: I was being lulled into a false sense of contentment by the surface so I wouldn't mind when the sea one day would swallow me whole.

III.

I don't think my culture deals very well with death. We mourn but we don't allow passion. We honor but we often forget to celebrate. When I grieve, I want to scream aloud. I want to be sick on the ground and to tear off my clothes and to puncture my arm with my own teeth and with sticks and pieces of broken glass. I want to find pictures of the deceased and wear them facedown under my clothes, next to my skin, until the photograph crumples and frays and the colors bleed all over me and bits of paper stick in my flesh. I want to jump up and down and shout their names over and over again and have everyone else who loved them jump up and down and shout their names so the ground will shake, and the air will move, and our voices will float off into space forever, and an alien a million years from now will catch it all in a jar and listen to the vibrations and hear their names repeated through some foreign sense. I want to laugh about every stupid thing they ever did and retell the story again and again. I want to keep every secret they ever told and at the same time write it out on a wall with spray paint in letters four feet high. I want to celebrate them and say thank you and thank you and thank you.

But usually we don't. We listen in shock; we remain strong; we cry a little; we choke on our pain; we dress up for a service; we wait to go numb. Sometimes. And sometimes, we have a wake.

The last time I saw Gary Edwards wasn't in Kodiak at all. It was in Seattle, at the train station. We'd had plans to spend the weekend at a pension neither of us could afford, to go to art museums and drink brandy and draw each other in the bathtub for a couple of days, but a storm delayed his plane in Philly where he was no doubt doing the same with another friend, and so I spent the weekend alone.

I was just heading home to Portland when I got his breathless call. He'd gotten into the airport and was racing to the station in a cab to say goodbye. We hugged and laughed for two minutes on the platform; he kept touching my ears and taking photographs from the hip, and then I was on the train and he was laughing again, waving dramatically and shouting, "Au revoir, Lara Lee! Au revoir!" Except that I would never see him again.

Gary's boat, the *Big Valley*, went down in the Pribilofs on January 15, 2005. I got the phone call the next day, and I remember my father's voice saying, "I have some very terrible news." His voice broke, and I only waited to hear which boat had sunk.

I remember saying, "NO NO NO NO NO NO NONONO-NONO." And then hanging up the phone. I spent the next few days glued to the internet, watching the headlines:

"Coast Guard Continues Search for Missing Crew."

"No Sign of Crabbers Missing at Sea."

"Search for Missing Crewmen Suspended."

"Sole Survivor of *Big Valley* Tragedy Conscious and Recovering after Extended Time in the Water."

"Times Announced for Pair of *Big Valley* Services."

I went back to Kodiak for the last time to attend. It was such a big deal that they held it in the high school auditorium to accommodate the mass of the gathering—friends and family of all of those lost, and Cache Seel—the miracle who survived. People spoke and shared stories and then shared food, but the whole ordeal felt too full of pain, too awkward. An opportunistic state representative showed up and took the mic and somehow managed to turn it into a plug for the soldiers in Iraq and was booed from the stage. A woman who had survived a shipwreck of her own tried to comfort me.

"It doesn't hurt, you know. Drowning. It's warm and you just go to sleep."

People said to me, "It's how he would have wanted it, to go down with his ship." Bullshit. Gary hated fishing. He had two phone lines just to avoid creditors, and most of his debt was in his boat. Where most crab boats boast cocaine and cans of spam and hustler center-folds, the *Big Valley* had an espresso machine, antique lithoprints on the walls, and coffee table books of Picasso and Matisse strewn around the galley. Gary wanted to die in Paris with a sketchbook and a nude model in his lap, not making what he swore was his "last trip" to the Pribs. That whole glory of the sea and the romance of the storm is a load of crap. It's cold, and it's huge, and they never find your body, so the people who love you have to let you go in other ways.

And so we did. Friends of Gary's—and he had so many, many friends, all of whom would call him their "best"—made their way to the only place any of us wanted to be, his home, part museum, part cultural center, part pleasure den. His captain's bed and drawings everywhere. Sculpture garden, a banya made from a wheelhouse, art made from stones and glass. We sat together for hours, telling stories, drinking, smoking. We built a bonfire in the yard higher than two of us on each other's shoulders. The ground was a slippery mass of frozen mud. Moe played the fiddle and someone else beat on the bottom of a plastic bucket, and people sang, and they stomped, and I had brought fire chains and spun flames around and around, and the fire burned higher and higher and the sparks whirled and we howled and we danced and loved them all: Gary and Josias and Aaron and Carlos and Danny.

That is a wake—to stand in the dark in a circle of people who love and to see clearly how a person has touched you, to wake up to their presence in your life, to their impact on others, and on the world. To let them burn through you so that that presence is awak-ened within you and you see how we are not in and of ourselves, but life moves through us together. And we say thank you and thank you and thank you.

17

Land

"WHERE ARE YOU FROM?" folks ask.

When I was in New York, I'd say, "the Pacific Northwest." When I was in Kodiak, I'd say, "New York," as if the answer always had to be far away.

Now I could say, "Well, we lived most of the year in Indiana when I was little, but we fished every summer out of Kodiak—though there was that one winter in Dutch Harbor—but then we moved to eastern Oregon, and we still fished in the summers, but we switched canneries, and then in my last couple of years on the boat we kind of drifted around, and then I went to college on the East Coast, and then I went overseas, and then San Francisco, and now I'm here and on my seventh address in Portland, and you know, my partner is from Chicago, so we go back to visit at least once a year. . . . Go Cubs!"

But I don't. Now that I'm settled down, I say "Alaska," and leave it at that. But it's not where I grew up, not really. Three months out of the year I traced the edges of an island. I've never been to Juneau, or Palmer, or Nome. I didn't walk the same cold road to and from school there. I didn't learn to take for granted the way the mountains and the water collide. I never got teased by older girls in the high school locker room in Kodiak or had crushes on teachers there. I didn't while away my days longing to leave.

But when the tide of homesickness floods, it's those waters that lap at my chest. It still gnaws at me like sand fleas on fresh bones on a beach, still whispers like dried grasses against my neck. The smell of salt water still makes the hair on my arms stand on end. I haven't fished in twenty years, but my body still knows seasons by its turns. Spring means the itch to go north, to think about gearing up or heading out. Summer means jellyfish and mosquitoes and fireweed smoking the hills. Fall is the time to return south.

Where am I from?

What do people want to know when they ask? Do they want to know where my accent comes from? Are they trying to guess how I dressed in high school, what music I liked? Are they picturing me as a child, playing on city streets, running in fields, picking stones on a beach, getting rides to the mall? I think what they really mean—what we all mean, when we ask—is, "Tell me more."

Or, "Why are you the way you are?"

So much of the way that I am comes from Alaska, from being on a boat. I can get myself out of bed to work when my body wants nothing more than to sleep. I carefully coil my garden hose. My husband always wants to let dirty pots soak overnight, and it drives me fucking crazy. "Just scrub the damn things harder!" I always say. Alaska taught me to work.

Alaska taught me a love and fear of the water. When people find out I'm not much of a swimmer, they always ask, "But didn't you grow up on a boat?" As if I'd been paddling canoes in the South Pacific, cavorting with dolphins. "Yeah," I answer, "and I tried not to fall off."

Alaska made me wary of men and their promises. Wives were out of sight and out of mind for so many that prowled the docks, and absence made the heart grow fonder for what was right in front of them.

Alaska made me hate being wet and cold. It made me love good rubber boots. And socks. Warm, dry socks. And food. Hot, plentiful food. I love sharp knives. Tidy knots. Stolen naps.

Alaska made me restless. Fishing is about seeking. It's about going after what you can't always see but what you hope is there—what you *know* is there. It's about chasing, and trying. And trying again, just because you can.

Alaska draws its own unto itself and sends the rest away. People go up there to find things: adventure, fortune, a sense of self—and either it gets their hooks in them and a summer gig turns into a life, or it spits them out, and people leave within weeks, saying "This isn't what I thought it was going to be." It's like having a master, or a mistress. I know myself best in relation to the incredible power that is there, the wildness and the aloof way the rocks and the bears and the waves and the water simply *don't care* about us. There is a whole piece of my identity that cannot be reflected by anything other than that: a self needs a mirror to remind it of its own contours or it disappears and grows weak, like smoke. There are parts of myself I only see, only recognize in the hands and the stories and the jokes of other fishermen. Of other women who fish.

I no longer go north, so I am often homesick: but for what? For long hours, uncomfortable bunks, hurried food? For aching muscles, sexual harassment, shitty sleep? Homesick for what community? The crews changed every year, sometimes every month, every closure. What faces? We barely saw the yellow and orange shapes of friends on faraway decks, their distant little Lego arms jerking a plunger or pawing at web. What place? A familiar river mouth, a favorite bay to anchor, a peak that looked different with every cloud that snagged on its pinnacle. Shifting, all of it was shifting—crews in and out, and fishing grounds rotating and canneries changing. None of it static, all of it escaping and in transition like tides.

Having no earth beneath your feet does something to you, to your mind, to your sense of self. The thing is: even when I was there, I felt that same longing and homesickness. It's not about missing a place, or a time, or community, it's what the *there* really is and means. It's the self that longs that is familiar, the seeking, restless self that is drawn. For me, that is the sweetest sense of home, the rootlessness, the lack of grounding.

I have traveled in strange places and have felt that wildness, that bigness, elsewhere. I was once in the middle of the desert—the desert of all deserts. The locals all slept through the brutal heat of midday, but I had wandered out into the shifting dry sea as if pulled by arid sirens, their voices full of hisses and quiet and promise. I waded over a ridge and then rested, lying against the side of a dune with the sun pounding down. The sand skittered over the surface and danced in light like pixies, like will-o'-the-wisp. The crystals caught the sun and tossed it in circles, making bright shapes I'd never seen, gently rubbing the skin from my fingertips, my face. There, a warm breath blew against my ear, full of a familiar sadness and longing that was profoundly familiar, at once pure longing and also something like being home. The space in between, knowing that there is, in fact, nothing to return to.

The last time I was in Alaska was for a funeral in 2005. I may never go back again. My child's middle name is Kodiak, and I gave them this name so that they would feel tied to the place, so they could discover it for themself in their own way, and find their own kind of meaning, their own unsettled lack of a home. I long to take them, but even as they paced the same boardwalks, ran along the same shale beaches clattering like coins, picked driftwood from the sand and breathed in the scents of salt, of gurry, of stone and wind and diesel and fiberglass, and heard the thrumming of the engine and the patter of seawater from the net as it dragged over the block—it would not be my home, would not be the same. There is nothing to return to but the memory. It is the longing that is familiar, not the place itself.

There is a word in Portuguese, *saudade*: a profound longing and feeling of sadness for someone or thing that is gone, lost, maybe never to return; one can even be in the presence of the person but feel a future or past disappear, and feel saudade—but inside the pain of saudade is also the joy of the love one feels for the thing or person, and the hope of consolation.

German has a word, *wehmut*: a wistfulness, a homesickness, yearning for the past. Romanian has *dor*, longing for someone or something loved, and the need to sing sad songs about it.

Welsh has *hiraeth*. Hiraeth is longing for home, but it is more than that. Pamela Petro says in her beautiful essay, "Dreaming in Welsh," "Home isn't the place it should have been. It's an unattainable longing for a place, a person, a figure, even a national history that may never have actually existed. To feel hiraeth is to feel a deep incompleteness and recognize it as familiar."

Where am I from?

I am from a place of longing. I am from the sea and its restlessness, from work and its temporary satisfaction. I am from the pleasure and pining for a home that may never have been.

Acknowledgments

This book would not exist without the encouragement and care of many people, particularly that of my family, Paul and Silas, who listen and read with patience, who make space for my work, and who make me laugh every single day; and of my parents, Jan and Stephanie Messersmith, who raised me in the wildest place imaginable.

I am also indebted to Moe Bowstern, for inviting me to the Fisherpoets Gathering and inspiring me to share my stories; to Jon Broderick, for giving me time on the stage; and to all the Fisherpoets who have cheered me on and shared stories over the years—your love and courage are everything.

I am grateful to my old critique group, The Guttery, for the challenging and thoughtful feedback that always made my work better: Jamie Yourdon, Cody Luff, Anatoly Molotkov, Tracy Manaster, Cameron Smith, David Cooke, Mo Daviau, Brian Reeves, Tammy Lynne Stoner, Kip Silverman, Carrie-Ann Tkaczyk, Bruce Greene, Michael Keefe, Jennifer Fleck, Robin Troche, Beth Marshea, Melanie Elisa, Margaret Pinard, and Susan DeFreitas.

A big thank-you to Tom Kizzia, my mentor at Fishtrap, for helping me rethink the role of journalistic integrity in creative nonfiction, and to the Regional Arts and Culture Council for the grant that allowed me to attend. Thank you to Vivian Faith Prescott and Chuck Smythe for guiding me to a better understanding of the sharing of clan stories. Thank you to the *Sou'Wester* for providing me with an artist's residency where I could focus on this work, and to all my friends who connect to it.

And lastly, thank you to master boatbuilder Ed Opheim, who is the origin of this book and who inspired a little girl to write, whether he knows it or not.

A version of chapter 4, "Wave," appeared under the title "Naming the Waves" in *Still Point Arts Quarterly* 34 (Summer 2019): 62–73. And a version of chapter 16, "Wake," appeared under the title "Three Wakes" in *Anchored in Deep Water: Gathering*, edited by Patrick Dixon and Chelsea Stephen, *The Fisherpoets Anthology* (2014): 30–34.

References

Aporta, Claudio. 2003. "Inuit Orienting: Traveling along Familiar Horizons." *Sensory Studies*. https://www.sensorystudies.org/inuit-orienting-traveling-along-familiar -horizons/.

Ashley, Clifford W., and Geoffrey Budworth. 1993. *The Ashley Book of Knots*. New York: Doubleday.

Broad, William J. 2017. "The Deep Seas Are Alive with Light." *Anchorage Daily News*, August 23, 2017. https://www.adn.com/alaska-news/science/2017/08/23/the-deep -seas-are-alive-with-light/.

Cartlidge, Edwin. 2015. "Physics May Reveal How to Tie the Perfect Knot." *Science Magazine | AAAS*, September 9, 2015. https://www.sciencemag.org/news/2015/09 /physics-may-reveal-how-tie-perfect-knot.

Cocker, Mark. 2020. "Michael Bond's Wayfinding: A Compelling Study of Our Ability to Get from A to B." *New Statesman* (UK). February 26, 2020. https://www .newstatesman.com/michael-bond-wayfaring-review.

"Communications (chapters 4–13)." n.d. Alaska History and Cultural Studies. http://www .akhistorycourse.org/articles/article_artID_178/.

Dauenhauer, Richard, and Nora Marks Dauenhauer. 2001. "The Salmon Story and Alaska Standards Activities & Suggestions." Edited by Juneau School District and Alaska Rural Systemic Initiative. Ankn.uaf.edu. June 2001. http://ankn.uaf.edu// ANCR/southeast/iamsalmon/SalmonStoryActivities.html.

Dobbs, David. 2017. "Are GPS Apps Messing with Our Brains?" *Mother Jones*, June 23, 2017. https://www.motherjones.com/media/2016/11/gps-brain-function-memory -navigation-maps-apps/.

Genz, Joseph H. 2016. "Resolving Ambivalence in Marshallese Navigation: Relearning, Reinterpreting, and Reviving the 'Stick Chart' Wave Model." *Structure and Dynamics* 9, no. 1. http://escholarship.org/uc/item/43h1d0d7.

Genz, Joseph, Jerome Aucan, Mark Merrifield, Ben Finney, Korent Joel, and Alson Kelen. 2009. "Wave Navigation in the Marshall Islands: Comparing Indigenous and Western Scientific Knowledge of the Ocean." *Oceanography* 22 (2): 234–45. https://doi .org/10.5670/oceanog.2009.52.

Horne, Francis. 2006. "How Are Seashells Created? Or Any Other Shell, such as a Snail's or a Turtle's?" *Scientific American*, October 23, 2006. https://www.scientificamerican .com/article/how-are-seashells-created/.

Kolbert, Elizabeth. 2006. "The Darkening Sea." *New Yorker*. November 12, 2006. https://www.newyorker.com/magazine/2006/11/20/the-darkening-sea.

Lachler, Jordan, Cherilyn Holter (T'áaw Kúns), Linda Schrack (Skíl Jádei), and Julie Folta. 2005. "Haida Cultural Emphasis: Chíin: Salmon." Edited by Annie Calkins. Sealaska Heritage. https://www.sealaskaheritage.org/Haida%20curriculum /PDFs/SALMON/Salmon_haida_booklet.pdf.

"Mail and Mail Carriers." n.d. National Postal Museum. https://postalmuseum.si.edu /exhibition/as-precious-as-gold-stories-from-the-gold-rush/mail-and-mail-carriers.

McCoy, Daniel. 2016. *The Viking Spirit: An Introduction to Norse Mythology and Religion*. North Charleston, SC: Createspace Independent Publishing Platform.

Melville, Herman. (1847) 2007. *Omoo: A Narrative of Adventures in the South Seas*. With an introduction and notes by Mary K. Bercaw. New York: Penguin Books.

National Geographic Society. 2013. "Bioluminescence." National Geographic Society. June 13, 2013. https://www.nationalgeographic.org/encyclopedia/bioluminescence/.

Nordquist, Richard. 2019. "Classic Essay on Observation: 'Look at Your Fish!'" ThoughtCo., July 21, 2019. https://thoughtco.com/look-at-your-fish-by -scudder-1690049.

"Northern Lights." n.d. Alutiiq Museum. https://alutiiqmuseum.org/word-of-the-week -archive/494-northern_lights.

Petro, Pamela. 2012. "Dreaming in Welsh." *Paris Review*, September 18, 2012. https:// www.theparisreview.org/blog/2012/09/18/dreaming-in-welsh/.

"Salmon Boy—a Haida Legend." 2019. First People. 2019. https://www.firstpeople.us /FP-Html-Legends/SalmonBoy-Haida.html.

Schneider, William S. 2012. *On Time Delivery: The Dog Team Mail Carriers*. Fairbanks: University of Alaska Press.

Skjalden. 2020. "Aegir and Ran—Norse Mythology." Nordic Culture. August 4, 2020. https://skjalden.com/aegir-and-ran/.

Snowden, Scott. 2019. "300-Mile Swim through the Great Pacific Garbage Patch Will Collect Data on Plastic Pollution." *Forbes*, May 30, 2019. https://www.forbes.com /sites/scottsnowden/2019/05/30/300-mile-swim-through-the-great-pacific-garbage -patch-will-collect-data-on-plastic-pollution/?sh=736979c7489f.

"The Edda & the Sagas of the Icelanders." n.d. Icelandic Literature Center. Accessed September 2021. https://www.islit.is/en/promotion-and-translations/icelandic -literature/the-edda-and-the-sagas-of-the-icelanders/.

Thomas, Marina. n.d. "Girl Who Married the Moon." Alutiiq Museum. https:// alutiiqmuseum.org/explore/past-exhibits/284-the-girl-who-married-the-moon52.

Tingley, Kim. 2016. "The Secrets of the Wave Pilots." *New York Times*, March 17, 2016. https://www.nytimes.com/2016/03/20/magazine/the-secrets-of-the-wave-pilots.html.

US EPA. 2016. "Effects of Ocean and Coastal Acidification on Marine Life." US EPA. September 8, 2016. https://www.epa.gov/ocean-acidification/effects-ocean-and -coastal-acidification-marine-life.

Zielinski, Sarah. 2013. "Animal Magnetism: How Salmon Find Their Way Back Home." NPR. February 7, 2013. https://www.npr.org/sections/thesalt /2013/02/07/171384063/animal-magnetism-how-salmon-find-their-way-back -home.